COUNTRY LIVING
M A G A Z I N E

MONTHS IN

THE COUNTRY

COUNTRY LIVING
M A G A Z I N E

B R I A N R E D H E A D

M O N T H S I N

T H E C O U N T R Y

𝔈

EBURY PRESS
LONDON

For Katy Brown

First published in 1992 by Ebury Press
an imprint of Random House UK Ltd
Random House
20 Vauxhall Bridge Road
London SW1V 2SA

Catalogue record for this book is available from the British Library.

ISBN 0 09 177517 5

The illustrations in the book are the work of Clare Leighton, a leading English wood-engraver. They are taken from her book *Four Hedges*, first published in 1935 and republished by Sumach Press in 1991.

EDITOR   *Katy Brown*
DESIGN   *Terry Jeavons*

Typeset by Hope Services (Abingdon) Ltd.
Printed and bound in Great Britain by Mackays of Chatham Plc, Kent

Contents

The first word
❧ ❧ ❧

IF ROOKS SAT on planning committees, no one would ever be allowed to chop down tall trees. "We need those," they would say, "as lodgings – so leave well alone. We have no plans to plant any more." That is the dilemma of wildlife. For creatures the countryside is simply a habitat, and they seek to make the best of it as it is, albeit in open conflict with other species.

Man is different. For him the countryside is an environment which he seeks, for better or for worse, to change. In the process he dislodges the others. Sometimes they move, but sometimes they have nowhere to go. We have made too much of a habit of destroying their habitat, and our world is diminished by their departure.

So what are we to do? Because to do nothing is not enough. Their survival depends upon us. Benign neglect on this over-crowded island will not save them. We cannot leave it simply to nature: we the clever ones, who can destroy, can also conserve.

Time is on our side, but not on theirs. If you say "Have a good day" to a mayfly, you are addressing its lifespan. It only has one day.

In an average life all mammals have almost the same number of breaths (200 million) and the same number of heartbeats (800 million). Small animals tick through life far more rapidly than large animals; their hearts beat more quickly and they breathe more frequently. Large animals live longer at a more stately pace. A whale sings so slowly that without a tape recorder to speed up the sound, a human being cannot even recognise it.

But measured by their own internal biological clocks, mammals of all sizes (unless they meet an untimely death) have the same lifespan. Some species simply get through it faster than others. Man, however, lives longer. His lifespan is 30 times greater than his size would suggest, so using his extra years he sets about rearranging the environment to suit himself.

Given the chance, other creatures would no doubt do the same, because this is not a battle between Man and Nature, it is one dominant species pushing the others aside. I imagine the rooks would like a country of tall trees. The moles would like a huge underground system, the platforms packed with worms.

They are not capable of making it happen, but Man is. He can alter the environment to suit himself and put the others in their place – meaning the place he has chosen for them, which may even be nowhere. His greeting to other creatures is either "Shove Up" or "Shove Off".

Not that every other creature always suffers when he alters the place for his own ends. The weeds and the pests, the scavengers and the opportunists often prosper – if only for a while. The seagulls thought they were on to a good thing with rubbish dumps and sewage outfalls until they began to die of botulism.

But unless Man thinks before he acts in the countryside, the wildlife will be the dispossessed. Building developments, pollution, intensive farming, afforestation, even recreational demands – all have robbed wildlife of somewhere to survive.

But we *can* improve things and we must. In this country we should not find it too difficult. Industry may have made a lot of mess in the last two centuries, but in spite of that, or perhaps because of that, we have a genuine love of the traditional country landscape. That was why intensive farming seemed so alien. It was not only an offence against the countryside, it was also an affront to our sympathies. The wildlife was pretty put out too.

If wildlife is to survive in Britain we need to graze meadows and moorland, manage woodlands and hedgerows, and excavate ponds. The creatures cannot do it for themselves. Only we can.

We must do it not because they have a right to survive (though they have), or because it is unfair to treat them badly (though it is), but because they are essential to our happiness. Man alone has the capacity to enjoy the environment and to marvel at the wonders of creation. We must not spoil our own enjoyment, or the rooks will look down on us.

1

Now
and
Always

———

The slow march forward
❦ ❦ ❦

THE ONLY THING this lot know about the ozone layer, said a Friend of the Earth at a recent gathering, is that it is above their heads.

He had a point. The discussion had lurched from subject to subject, but almost all the speakers had felt the need to raise their eyes to the heavens and mention That Hole. It was, it seemed, the sign of the true faith.

This was a green gathering and we were there to discuss the future of the countryside, a big enough subject in itself you might think, but for many of those present it was not enough. They appeared to be divided between Roundheads and Cavaliers. For the Roundheads it was all or nothing – Planet Earth not just mountains green. Not for them the replaced hedgerow or the rescued pond. They wanted a New Earth.

The Cavaliers, who were in a minority, appeared to accept that there is more than enough to cope with near at hand, but even they would not settle for one thing at a time. They galloped hither and thither and the list of their demands, if accepted, would occupy our legislators until the end of the next century.

They wanted a Ministry of Environmental Protection and more money for all the conservation agencies. They wanted to curb the powers of British Coal and even more of any privatised body that might succeed it. And they wanted no more privatisation of anything.

They wanted lower taxes in rural areas, complete protection for the Green Belt, a lower permitted density of infill, and no reduction in rights of way.

They wanted less traffic on the roads and more on the railways, a lower speed limit and more bicycles. They wanted alternative power stations, pay-as-you-pollute taxation, and strict controls of noise pollution.

They wanted to help organic farmers, to encourage small-holdings, and to camouflage hay bales. Oh, and something must be done urgently about That Hole. More, more, shouted the Roundheads adding their chorus.

We must protect all species and their habitats, ban all products from rain forests, halt offshore dumping, discourage over-population, respond to rising sea-levels, stop the global warming.

Stop the world, I want to get off, said my Friend of the Earth, and we adjourned to the bar. He was very melancholy. They drive me mad, he said. One lot make an evergrowing list of what needs to be done, without indicating in what order and why. And the other lot want to be God.

My, you've changed, I thought, though I did not say so out loud. Five years ago you would have been a ranter too, asking for everything at once. Now you want to see things happen rather than hear things said.

So I suggested that we made a list of what was changing for the better and what we could reasonably expect to change quite soon. The result was nothing like as long or as majestic as the list of demands, let alone as disturbing as the list of recent damage. But nonetheless, slowly and reluctantly, he began to agree that we are making progress.

There is now an increasing awareness that the environment must be protected, locally, nationally, and globally. And things are happening – whether by international agreement, national legislation, or local activity.

There are still countless offenders, but they are now seen to be offensive and penalties are being exacted. Silly decisions in favour of unwelcome developments are being overturned, and before long instead of objectors having to argue why something should not happen, developers will be compelled to argue why it should.

Presumptions are changing. Ten years ago in this country there was talk of discarding all planning controls. Now there is talk only of the restoration of planning.

No one believes any longer that the safety of the environment can be left to chance, or to market forces. It is true that the villains still multiply, but their villainy is both detected and denounced. And there is more interest in wildlife than there has ever been.

It still doesn't add up to very much, he said.

Yes, I said, but it is a start. The environment for the environment has changed. What was previously tolerated is now deemed intolerable. What was previously unthinkable is now said openly.

What was eccentric is now central.

But it is not very dramatic, he said.

That, I said, quoting myself, is because it is peace not war. War is dramatic and noisy and damaging, like the threats to the environment. The good things are gentle, quiet, conserving. And you have to work at them.

I will, I will, he said, perking up at last. After all, the need to protect the environment is no longer a fad or a fashion, it is a fact of life, he said in the voice of one for whom the penny has dropped, and you can quote me.

So I have.

Curse of the cobblestones

❦ ❦ ❦

HER LETTER ARRIVED the morning after I had attended a conference on the future of the countryside. The arguments had been
very familiar, the indignation somewhat simulated. This would
have made them sit up, I thought.

The letter was from a woman who was born in the country,
on the edge of the same fell in the north of England where her
ancestors settled six centuries ago. She grew up and went to
school there and she wished the same for her children. But when
tourism forced up house prices in the country she was alone
with young children and could not afford a house there, so she
had to move to a town where she could afford a home.

She was horrified by the callousness and rootlessness of the
town, and for 10 years threw her house open to every youngster
who needed a roof, a meal, or a shoulder to weep on.

Not being a driver, she rarely saw her native fells and becks.
Can you imagine, she wrote, the agony of not hearing the
curlews return and wheel in the darkness in that first spring
night of mating on the wind, not smelling the hay and honey-
suckle in the deep lanes, never feeling the brown river water
slipping like warm silk over your shoulders, never seeing the red
fox sloping home in the dawn, or tasting inky mushrooms drip-
ping with dew?

But when her father died someone had to be on hand to
help with her mother, who was arthritic, and with the children
now through school and self-supporting, she went back.

Things were not what they had been. The planning authority
had, as she put it, planted their battle standards on the boundaries and a working village had become a dormitory town and a
tourist complex.

Ugly signboards and stiles barricaded the old footpaths.
Farmers who used to welcome and pass the time of day with
casual walkers had security-fenced their fields into no-go areas.

Vast queues of traffic made the roads unsafe for walking and cycling. The fluorescent clothing of the hordes of walkers and enthusiasts, who could not see beyond the facilities for their own sport, scarred the green fells and scared the shy wildlife.

One of her adopted children from the town said the village was full of football hooligans and lager louts and he was too scared to stay.

And the village itself had changed. Blocks of luxury apartments had replaced the bakery, the blacksmith's, several farms and several old mills, and many shops. There was no longer a grocer. And, would you believe, she said, cobblestones had been laid picturesquely to ruin the village street for all practical purposes?

Even the local poacher had dried out and retired to the sanctuary of a tent in the vicarage garden, and then retreated even further to a wardrobe in the woods.

Nonetheless, she was happy to be back. Her mother has an acre of pasture adjoining the house, on which once stood her grandfather's workshop (he was a joiner) plus various henhouses, kennels, and a greenhouse. They have all been demolished but the footings remain, so the planning authority allowed her to put a trailer there provided she used the kitchen and bathroom in the house. A high hedge screened the trailer from the road.

But then one day a new planning officer arrived saying that he had received complaints about the "new access" to the field. She pointed out that there had always been access to the field to let in stock and tractors and haymaking machinery and it was in the deeds.

But what, he asked, are you doing here without planning permission? She pointed out that she had permission from his predecessor, that the trailer was parked on the foundations of an earlier building, that it was not static and had no services. Furthermore just over the hedge, in what used to be the old station yard, there was now a coal and builder's supply yard with trailers and touring vans. But this field, said the planner, is agricultural land, not to be used for other purposes.

To cut a long argument short she moved her trailer into her mother's garden, which is within the curtilage of the house, so as not to be accused of destroying "agricultural" land, although quite what her grandfather, the joiner, would have made of that is difficult to imagine.

She has now been told that her trailer can remain where it is as long as she does not live in it. On its new site it is easily visible from all directions and positively mars the orchard, but it can stay there and, as she wrote, rust and rot and deface the countryside.

All this, she agrees, would be no more than a little local difficulty were it not that conversations with other locals have revealed, or so she says, that it is the oldest families who are being harried and dogged, presumably in the hope that they will give up their ancestral acres which are ripe for development.

Some of them have even told her that the only way to avoid such harassment is to line a pocket or two, a point I would have pooh-poohed had I not heard the same complaint from an aggrieved farmer.

And certainly my correspondent is very cross. She has now heard that a mile down the road, along the edge of what she describes as the deepest, greenest, leafiest, bluebelliest, shadiest country lane, they are to cover two huge water-meadows along the loveliest curve of the river with industrial units.

Ah well, she says, I still know a bank whereon the hemlock grows.

A frog's life

I WOULD NOT like to be a frog in February. I suspect that I would not like to be a frog at any time of year, though I can see that life could have its moments in midsummer, when I would a-wooing go. But not in midwinter.

Frogs spend their winters with their heads down. They lie torpid in the mud in the bottom of ponds, waiting for better days. When the ponds freeze over there is always a danger of some fool skating on the ice. The vibrations from his gyrations shake the frogs from their slumbers and they rise to the surface and bang their heads. It is a rude awakening, and they can seldom get back to sleep.

A pond is not a plaything. It is somebody's home, and it is up to us both to create that home and to look after it. Because most ponds are, and always have been, man-made.

Oliver Rackham, who knows about ponds, reckons that the oldest man-made pond in England is probably the one called Point Pond which is in Great Ridge Wood near Salisbury. He says that pond was first dug before the Bronze Age, by a Stone Age man.

Britain was once covered in ponds, and even today there are no fewer than 340,000 ponds in England and Wales, not counting those in people's back gardens. But 100 years ago there were 800,000 ponds, 14 to the square mile. London has lost 95 per cent of its ponds in the last 100 years. They have simply been filled in to make way for buildings and roads – and that has happened in every town and city.

In the country, ponds die of neglect. If no one tends them they silt up. They get shallower and shallower as the vegetation piles up and rots, and they get darker and darker as the surrounding vegetation becomes overgrown. No frog in its right mind, and no fish, insect or bladderwort for that matter, wants to live in dark, dank squalor.

Ponds which are neither in the town or the country, but in the fringe territory between, are often the worst done-by. They are not only neglected but they are used as rubbish tips. All of which is unfair to frogs, who have become homeless refugees in their own country. What they need, and what we need, is a big pond-building programme.

A pond should be dug at least two feet deep, and the bigger the better. It should be an irregular shape, with gentle sloping sides and a shallow end for those plants which like to keep their heads above water.

There are, or so I am told, three ways of lining a pond. It can be lined with puddled clay, rather like lining a pie dish. This takes a lot of clay and a lot of patience but it is cheap and lasts a long time, and the frogs love it. A pond can be lined with concrete, which is also cheap, fits any shape, and is durable. But frogs don't really like concrete ponds any more than human beings like high-rise flats. They are not comfortable. The third method is to have a flexible lining, and there are two schools of thought on how best to do this. Some say you should line the pond with old carpet and newspapers sandwiched between two sheets of polythene. But others say that you should simply line the pond with sand or sawdust or old carpet and cover it with one sheet of polythene. You dig a trench around the rim, lay the edge of the polythene sheeting in it, and cover it with earth. You have to leave the sheeting fairly slack because the weight of the water causes it to stretch.

Myself, I favour the puddled-clay method, though to be honest I have never built a pond. The one I owned, I inherited.

But however you choose to line the pond, you need to stock it with plants. You need submerged root plants, things like water-crowfoot and starwort and hornwort. You need floating-leaved plants like broadleaved pondweed and white and yellow waterlilies. You need emergent plants, of which there are many, including bur reed, reed mace, arrowhead and lesser spearwort. You also need a few marginal plants like pond sedge and water mint and creeping buttercup. But don't have anything to do with Canadian pondweed because it gets everywhere.

Put in some water snails but don't stock it with fish because they have no sense of neighbourliness and eat all the invertebrates. So too do bladderworts, which are carnivorous aquatic plants. But you can have a world of aquatic life including water fleas that don't bite; stick-insects, spiders, dragonflies, waterboatmen. You can support newts, and if the pond is deep enough even the Great Crested Newt, who in spite of his triumphal name is very shy and likes to court in dense weed.

And you will have frogs. They need no invitation. They will make their own way to your water, glad of somewhere decent to live. And when they arrive, don't call them toads.

Toads too are tail-less leaping amphibians, but they prefer to live on land. They are shorter and squatter than frogs and not as strong in the legs. They also have rough, dry and warty skins.

I would definitely not like to be a toad, at any time.

Green but not heard
❦ ❦ ❦

HE WAS SITTING in a cardboard box, not a million miles from
Whitehall, muttering to himself. Most passers-by did not even
spare him a glance, but I paused, curious to know what he was
on about. What we need, he said, glowering, is not a
Department *of* the Environment but a Department *for* the
Environment.

To build you a house? I said.

No, you fool, he replied. Quite the opposite.

Then I recognised him.

You used to have a job in the Department of the
Environment, I said.

He nodded, grimaced and clambered to his feet.

I led him across the road, not to the first pub but (remembering that he prefers real ale) to the second. And, once settled,
he told me about his discontent. You will remember, he said,
that the Department of the Environment grew out of the
Ministry of Housing and Local Government.

I remember very well, I said. I was a planning correspondent in the early Sixties when town planning was everything.
You either got a new town centre or a New Town. And everyone was talking about local government reform.

They are again, he said. He took another drink and leant
forward.

What you must understand, he said to me, is that in
Whitehall those who are green are not heard.

Did you know that the chap who wrote the White Paper on
the Environment a couple of years ago (which, if not a plan of
action, was at least a declaration of intent), had to spend many
months knee deep in the successor to the poll tax?

Now, I am not suggesting for a moment that the reform of
local government and of local government finance is unimpor-
tant, even if it is largely the correction of errors which ought
never to have been committed in the first place. But the fact

remains that if this is now the number one priority in the Department — and it is — then we have to ask: who now *will* look after the environment? Lots of people, I said, beginning to recite a list of quangos and royal societies and devoted trusts. But he cut me off.

They all do good things, I know, he said, and do so increasingly in partnership, but you know as well as I that the government always has the final word, and if it does not take the environment seriously — hard luck on the environment.

He paused for a moment.

Do you know what finally persuaded me to stand up and be counted? he asked. An opinion poll published at the start of National Environment Week, which revealed that British schoolchildren are resigned to inheriting a polluted and damaged world.

What do you want then? I asked. A new government agency?

No, he said, we have very good agencies up and down the country looking after their bit of the environment. What we need in addition is a Department *for* the Environment, as powerful and influential as the Treasury or the Foreign Office.

The present Department should concentrate on local government and be known as the Department of Local Government.

The new Department for the Environment would have the final say both on what ought not to happen and what should be encouraged to happen in the environment.

Perhaps, I said, the Prime Minister, as well as being First Lord of the Treasury, should also become First Lord of the Environment.

Many a true word, he said. The truth is that the time has come for us to make up our minds about whether or not we are serious about matters green. The environment is not simply a dimension of life, it is the condition of living.

You are getting philosophical, I said. Perhaps you should live in a barrel, as Diogenes did, not in a cardboard box.

Let us empty this one, he said. Then I shall decide.

Watch the worm
☙ ☙ ☙

WILL YOU PUT in a word for the worm? asked a friend of Country
Living, egged on I suspect by a green-fingered small son.

Charles Darwin beat me to it, I replied. He considered the
earthworm to be the most important animal in the history of the
world.

But not everyone agrees.

The worm is not only overlooked but undervalued. The very
word, whether used as a noun or as a verb, is dismissive. Even a
worm will turn, we sneer. He wormed himself in, we hiss.

All of which is very unfair. A worm may turn, but it will
never turn nasty. And the garden would be lost without them.

It is estimated that the worm population in the average
herbaceous garden is about a quarter of a million per hectare,
which is roughly a hundred thousand per acre. And as Gilbert
White, the 18th-century naturalist, said, without worms the
earth would soon become cold, hardbound, void of fermentation
and consequently sterile.

What worms do is tunnel through the earth. Although they
have no bones or skeleton, they are very strong. All segments
and bristles, they can anchor one end while pushing themselves
forward with the other.

The maze of tunnels they create constantly aerates and drains
the soil. But they do not simply push their way through: they
eat their way through, digesting any organic material as they go.
In effect, they both turn over the soil and fertilise the soil.

The common earthworm can be anything from four inches
to a foot long, and many people claim to have seen worms 20
inches long, but that may be stretching a point.

Not that we need worms to be giants to be seduced by
them. The first World Worm Charming Championships, I recall,
were held at Willaston, near Nantwich in Cheshire, in July
1980. A local farmer's son, Tom Shufflebotham, who was then

20, charmed 511 worms out of the ground in half an hour. He did it by gently vibrating the soil, coaxing the worms to the surface. A great feat.

Perhaps you would like to take up worm charming, or at least worm watching. March is the month when they begin to venture forth, having spent much of the winter lining their tunnels with fallen leaves.

They emerge at dawn and in the evening, for they are not wholly subterranean in their habits. No more are they carefree. They keep one end firmly in the ground while the other end explores the surface looking for anything organic.

They drag what they find into the tunnel, eat some of it and deposit the rest, which then rots and helps to feed the plants. But all the time they forage they are alert, ready to withdraw instantly at the first hint of danger.

If you want to observe them as the light fades you must walk very carefully becuse they are very sensitive to vibrations and will shoot back into their tunnels at the slightest tremor.

I confess I cannot really see worm watching catching on as a mass pursuit with worm watcher clubs and organised field visits, but I did hear of an infants' school where the worm has joined the tadpole as a creature for study.

And a friend in Scotland swears that he once heard a sermon preached on the wonders of creation in which the minister made much of the sanctity of the earthworm and even speculated on whether every earthworm is an individual.

That in turn apparently provoked a great argument afterwards among the students who had been in the congregation, with much quotation of Darwin and some rumblings among the creationists present.

Eventually an old gentleman who had been listening with much amusement to their discussion said that what mattered was not whether the earthworm has an immortal soul but whether it has a purpose. And they all agreed that it has. But that is true of all creatures great and small, not least the worm.

The north-south frontier

❦ ❦ ❦

HISTORY IS WHAT people make of their geography, and nowhere is that more evident than in the north of England. In the simplest geographical terms England is like Scotland; it is divided into the highlands and the lowlands. The north is the highlands; it is that part of England which is dominated by the Pennines. The south is the rest. And that is the north-south divide.

The frontier between the north and the south is a line drawn from the Humber to the Dee. It is not a straight line; it curves down and round to embrace the Peak District.

If you are driving from south to north then once you reach Ashbourne in Derbyshire you have arrived. But as you lift your eyes to the hills, you must not leap to the wrong conclusion.

There are no fewer than five National Parks in the north and that is an appropriate recognition of its natural beauty, but it can lead to a misunderstanding of its history.

The beautiful parts of the north are no more unoccupied territory than are the industrial conurbations, and that is all the more reason for knowing them and for looking after them. They are monuments to nature and to man – living monuments.

The whole of the north of England is a lived-in and a lived-on landscape, and it has been for 10,000 years and more. Wherever you go in the north, from high level to sea level, someone has been there before. And not all of them have done damage. The remotest areas were once someone's home and the hills were always hospitable. The evidence would suggest that people lived in the hills before they lived on the plains. When the Celts arrived from the Continent and climbed and named Cheviot they were taken aback to discover that others had beaten them to it. Their graves were there to prove it.

Successive peoples took to the hills, and it was centuries before the people followed their fortunes downstream, beckoned by water power into a head of steam.

That is recent history. The joy of the north is that what happens now can be seen to be a consequence of what went before. It is, for example, a curious fact that the most prosperous towns in the north now are those which were founded by the Romans. Clearly they knew a good place when they saw one.

In the north there is not a past and a present, but rather an ever-changing present. Its history is not what people made of the geography, but what people make of it now.

Stand on any piece of high ground in the north and look around, and you will see the then and the now and the always. I remember, for example, one day a few years ago, standing on the platform at Ribblehead station, which is the most dramatic halt on the Carlisle-Settle railway line.

It struck me then that everything there is, and could only be, in the north – not least of course the place itself, high up in the Pennines. The railway line was the last great line north, the best engineered, and still the most argued over.

The path from west to east once carried the monks from Furness Abbey to Rievaulx Abbey. The path from south to north is the Pennine way, opened after a great campaign 30 odd years ago, and now the most frequented walk in the land.

On that day I recall they were busy extending the quarry alongside the railway line to provide limestone for a new process to limit pollution from power stations and there was much dissension. But there was general agreement that it was a good idea to restore the ruins of 18th-century mills as ruins, for they were thought to be every bit as attractive and interesting as ruined abbeys.

And it was thought even better that the oldest and biggest industrial building down that valley was being converted then into workshops for a dozen new crafts.

This, I thought at the time, is a lived-in landscape, busier perhaps than it has ever been before, but still beautiful, remote, and fought over.

That, I submit, is the very nature of the north.

One man, one acre

🍂 🍂 🍂

IT IS ALL very well for you living in the north, said a letter from an old lady in Hampshire, to say that when you look round you can see the then and the now and the always. But from where I look, all I can see is the now.

And she went on to explain that when she and her late husband bought their house just after the Second World War, using his army gratuity as a deposit, they were on the edge of the village looking out across hay meadows.

She still lives in the same house but now she looks out across a junior executive housing estate, with not a hayrick or a hedgerow in sight. I sometimes think, she wrote, that there is no room for any more people. She has a point.

It is one thing to put up a notice at the entrance to the Lake District on a Bank Holiday Monday saying "FULL", when you know the visitors will go home at bedtime.

It is quite another to put up a notice at the entrance to Hampshire on any day of the year saying "FULL", when you know the inhabitants are there to stay – and more want to move in.

And more, according to my correspondent in Hampshire, means worse. That, she hastened to add, is not a judgement on the newcomers but on the impact of their arrival.

I know, she said in her letter, that I sound like the Mad Hatter (or was it the March Hare?) endlessly repeating "No Room, No Room", but I really think it is true. What can be done about it is another matter. People have to have somewhere to live, but why here?

The answer to the last question, I suppose, is the estate agent's typical answer: it is a highly *desirable* place. But it is not a satisfactory answer.

There are roughly 56 million people in this country and this country is roughly 56 million acres. If all things were equal we would have an acre each, plus perhaps a cow and a beanstalk.

But things are not equal. From the year dot to the year 1900 we built on two million of those 56 million acres. Between 1990 and 1950 we built on another two million acres. In other words, we covered as much land in the first half of this century as we had in all previous centuries.

And since 1950, in spite of, or perhaps because of, planning controls, we have gone mad. When the acres covered are added up at the end of the century they will have to publish them in hectares to make them look fewer.

Everyone who wants to build something new is looking for land. But there is no such thing as new land, or more land; the only change is in the use of land.

For too long it was assumed that new development required green field sites. There are regions of Britain where, between 1950 and 1980, agricultural land was being built on at the rate of 100 acres a week. Then someone pointed out that developers could look inward as well as outward. Land which had been used once could be used again.

About a decade ago, I recall, the regional economic planning council in the north-west of England discovered that its region led the country in dereliction. It had used and spoiled more land than any other region of Britain. It had 25,000 derelict, despoiled, or vacant areas. But how, they asked, will we persuade people to build upon them afresh?

I suggested one answer to the then Secretary of State for the Environment. Why not designate all derelict land "Green Belt", I said, then we shall not be able to move for property developers trying to get permission to build on it? In the event they came up with other inducements, and in addition were shamed into it.

It makes no sense to go on expanding the built-up area at the expense of the countryside while at the same time leaving dereliction behind. It might be easier to develop green field sites but it is clearly irresponsible.

And so they set about clearing up not only the mess of previous centuries but more recent errors too. In the process more and more people are rediscovering the pleasures of city-dwelling, moving back in, instead of moving further out. All this is not to deny people the joys of country living, but to make sure that suburbia no longer dribbles into the countryside.

Built-up Britain is big enough. We can accommodate the population without further resource to *overspill* – the very word suggests careless error. The task now is to correct the mistakes of the past and to create towns in which people choose to live, not from which to flee.

The countryside is something else. Somebody said – and I think it was me – that we need city life to prove that we are civilised and we need country life to prove that we are whole.

The whole population cannot live in the country, nor would it want to. But everybody needs to know that the countryside is intact – cherished, not plundered. Now and always.

2

Every
Village

A sense of belonging

❦ ❦ ❦

HAVE YOU NOTICED . . . perhaps I had better say this in a whisper not to offend those who may take it personally . . .

Have you noticed how many houses with little brown windows are springing up all over the country? You see them everywhere — on old sites and in green fields, on the outskirts of towns and on the edge of villages — wherever the developers choose to strike. They are not a sign of age, like brown spots on old hands, but a sign of the age — instant, like the language of the marketing man. And they are certainly not in the vernacular.

I first came across the expression "vernacular architecture" many years ago when I was introduced to the man who knows most about it in Britain, R W Brunskill. Let me guess, I said, vernacular architecture swears at the clients. Speaks out, he replied. And he went on to explain, as he has in his many books on the subject, that vernacular architecture has much in common with language. It is not polite speech; but equally it is not offensive. It is local, like dialect; but it is not vulgar, like abuse.

Great imposing buildings — places of assembly, of worship, of celebration — are not the only works of architecture in the land. Many small buildings — houses, barns, windmills — untouched by architects are works of architecture too, but of vernacular architecture.

They are not just any old place. No more are they splashes of speculative development. But they have, to use Pevsner's famous phrase, the same "conscious aesthetic intention" as any fine building. They also have something else: they belong. They belong to the district where they are found and to no other.

They satisfy the simple demands of the family life, or of the farming ways, or of the industrial processes of the locality. They use traditional designs, which are subject to gradual change, and they are built of materials near to hand. That is the vernacular.

Great architecture is more politely spoken, more academic,

more refined, the language of the educated everywhere. It has grand designs, universal concepts, great abstractions.

The vernacular is more down to earth, more concrete, more practical. To understand it you need to understand the dialect, which is not simply a vocabulary but a language, a tradition of speech. Knowledge of the words is not in itself enough. You need to know what to say and when to say it.

Any fool can read a cookery book, but only a practised cook can bake a good pie. Vernacular architecture is like that. It is home cooking. Grand architecture is *haute cuisine*. The little brown windows are convenience food.

To prefer the vernacular to the new development is not nostalgia. It is like preferring home-made trifle to instant whip. It is a preference for what is better. To continue to build in the vernacular is not to live in a museum but to work in a tradition. Just as the cook will swop the open grate for the Aga, so the builder will swop the pick and shovel for the JCB. But the essentials can still be the same. Stone is still stone, timber is still timber. We can still have ridge purlins and catslide roofs, lattices and mullions, whatever belongs.

It is not a matter of following slavishly what went before (there is more slavery in following fashion); it is a matter of preferring the permanent to the temporary. Junk building, like junk food, is instantly disposable. We are already knocking down the errors of recent decades while trying desperately to conserve the emblems of recent centuries.

We have in this country the world's finest collection of traditional buildings, and I think we should build some more. You can shout that from the rooftops.

Carbuncular housing

❦ ❦ ❦

ONE MONDAY MORNING a few years ago, I found myself in an empty village. It was a sparkling day in summer, and the village, which was no more than a cluster of stone cottages around a green, could not have looked better. But there was nobody there, not a single living soul, not even a cat.

Consumed by the thought that it must have been like this during the Black Death, I walked round wondering why it was deserted, and then it dawned on me. This was a village of second homes, all locked, secure, and unoccupied from Monday to Friday – which may be nice for the weekenders, but is no substitute for village life.

Very few villages are wholly or largely second homes. I have come across only two, one in the Cotswolds and one in the Yorkshire Dales, which appear to be deserted during the week. But there are many where the second homes are beginning to equal or even to outnumber the homes of the local residents. In one country area of Derbyshire, there were 100 holiday homes at the last census. Seven years later there were 400.

Fewer and fewer local people can buy the houses in the villages in which they were born and brought up. They simply cannot afford them, with the result that there is not only a social imbalance but social deprivation. Villages lose schools, post offices, shops, and other services because of the shortage of a resident population. Weekenders do not send their children to the village school.

In the Lake District the Special Planning Board tried to do something about it. In the National Park as a whole they discovered that 10 per cent of the houses were holiday homes and unoccupied for large parts of the year. In the centre of the Park the figure went up to 20 per cent, and in the really popular places it was between 30 and 40 per cent.

Enough is enough, they proclaimed. So they tried to make it

a rule that new housing would be sold only to the local people, but the Government would have none of it. Indeed the Environment Secretary at the time got quite shirty. "Conditions should not be imposed on planning permissions for private dwelling houses," he said, "which have the effect of depriving householders of their normal rights to sell or let their houses to whomsoever they wish . . . Planning control is essentially concerned with the use and development of land, not with the identity or characteristics of the user." So there.

The Westmorland Gazette, the newspaper founded by Wordsworth and first edited by De Quincy, was furious. "A bleak and unsettled future," it said, "faces young people in the Lake District as a result of the Government's decision . . . The result can only be that generations of youngsters who have been brought up in Lakeland villages will be forced into towns on the edge of the National Park. It makes nonsense of attempts to provide rural jobs."

That was a few years ago, and since then the argument has raged throughout the National Parks. Instead of insisting that new houses should be sold only to local people, some Parks tried the argument that they be sold only to people who at least would use them as their sole or main residence. The Secretary of State vetoed that too.

Others even argued that the answer might be simply to refuse all applications for new housing. And although that was thought to be a trifle negative, there is no doubt that all future applications in National Parks for new housing are going to have to satisfy a great many conditions, of which the most important will be what is the advantage for the local community.

The next Minister of the Environment's view was very simple. He said that if there was a shortage of housing for local people then build some more. But it is not quite as easy as that. A new housing estate was built in Keswick in 1972. When the houses were eventually sold it was discovered that 44 were occupied by incoming retired people, 25 were bought as holiday homes, and only 20 served the local need. The truth is that if new houses are desirable residences they are snapped up by incomers either as retirement homes or holiday homes, and if they are not very desirable they disfigure the landscape. Nothing is more depressing than a village with a suburban accretion, a row of semi-detached houses, pebble dashed and dashed off, wholly out of character with the original dwellings.

If villages are to expand to accommodate more people then it is important that the new buildings are in sympathy with the old. And new additions should not alter the character of the village as a whole. The village I live in is a necklace of hamlets, and the local authority wisely rejected a plan to insert a housing development which would have sat on its neck like a carbuncle.

A *Country Living* reader in Wiltshire is not so lucky. She sent me a map of her village where the lane on which she lives has nine entrances to nine houses with 15 cars in 200 yards – more than enough development you would think. But now, by taking advantage of a planning permission granted 30 years ago but not taken up until now, the lane has been "backfilled". There is a tenth entrance leading to a new development of several four bedroomed "executive" houses which will cover the south-facing slope behind the existing houses which was their principal delight.

It is a sad and sorry affair, she wrote, and so common in our villages today. She is right. There is too much of it, and there will be more as land unwanted for farming is made available for development.

A housing estate is not a village. A village needs a past as well as a future. It can grow but it must not be forced – nor left empty.

The centre of the village

❦ ❦ ❦

THE SCARECROW WAS unhappy.

Would you like it, he said, stuck out here on your own, week in week out, scarcely ever seeing a living soul?

But I thought the birds dropped in, I said.

Dropped on you mean, he replied, shuddering.

So where would you prefer to be? I asked.

Down there, he said, on the village green.

But I thought, I said, that you were meant to be a warning.

Precisely, he replied.

Follow me, I said, and we walked down to the village green, he, it has to be admitted, a trifle stiffly.

When we got there a small crowd swiftly gathered, and he turned to address the multitude. At that moment the church clock struck 11.

Are you aware, he said, that this green is older than that church, and that church is Saxon. You have looked after the church but you have let them ruin the green.

There is still grass, said a voice.

Only just, he said. Look at that monstrosity, and that, and that, and that . . .

His arm moved in a series of angry jerks as he pointed to the things he disapproved of.

The hideous bus shelter with its broken windows.

The clutch of litter bins, strewn with split plastic bags.

The road gravel bin with its missing lid and most of its contents spilled.

The road sign which someone had twisted so that it pointed in the wrong direction.

The no-parking sign, and the broken down car beside it.

The telegraph pole with its dangling wires.

And the metal billboard with its torn posters.

Ugh, he said.

But that is the rotten end of the village green, said a voice, the other end is much tidier.

The scarecrow turned full circle.

Suburban, he said, dismissing the endeavours of the parish council with a single gesture.

Clearly he was not impressed by the neatly mown grass, trimmed with curbstones, defined by iron chains, and decorated with a single sign saying Keep Off.

At that moment there was a squeal of brakes and the angry blowing of a car horn. It was also a mistake to build a road right across the middle of the village green, said the scarecrow.

But we have to be able to get to the by-pass, said a voice.

The scarecrow groaned.

And we have to be able to drive to the Leisure Centre, said a young man who looked like a lollipop.

The scarecrow muttered something to himself, an oath perhaps, or a prayer.

What you must understand, he said, is that the village green should not be abused, but it should be enjoyed. We want no foolish installations but equally we want no silly prohibitions.

We want people to enjoy the use of the green as they have for the last 12 centuries. We want the little ones to play on it, their older brothers to compete on it, the elders to sit and watch on it.

This is the place for morris dancers and the maypole, for fireworks and the bonfire, for Christmas carols and pancake races. This is the centre of the village and it should be the centre of village life.

An elderly woman, who had listened to his every word, approached the scarecrow.

It used to be like that when I was a young girl, she said. It was ours, but it does not seem to be ours any longer. What can we do?

Register the green, replied the scarecrow.

The old lady looked puzzled.

I thought all village greens were registered, she said.

Sadly not, said the scarecrow, who had donned a wig.

The 1965 Commons Registration Act allowed land to be registered as a village green but the registration period was far too short. If the green was not registered by July 1970 it was too late. And land which was not registered failed to have any legal status as a green from August 1970.

But, he went on gravely, the 1965 Act provides for the registering of new village greens by actual use of the land by local people for lawful sports and pastimes for at least 20 years. So, on land previously unregistered, a new 20 years' use was built up by August 1990.

All you have to do is to prove it has been used as a green these past 20 years.

These past twelve hundred and twenty years, added the old lady.

Well, said the scarecrow, registration is certainly the best protection against development threats, misuse, and any other encroachment.

At that moment the church clock struck 12.

The old lady thanked the scarecrow and signalled to the elders in the crowd to join her in the village pub. Clearly a decision was about to be taken.

Should I walk you back? I said to the scarecrow.

No, he said, I think I shall go to the pub with them. For a stiff one.

Know your place

❦ ❦ ❦

PLEASE, WROTE AN anguished correspondent, can you do something to stop them closing our village school?

Please, wrote another, can you do something to stop them developing an agricultural industrial estate alongside our village?

Please, wrote a third, can you do something to stop them building executive houses on a very special piece of land?

All three pleas arrived in the same post, and they were not for my eyes alone. Copies had been sent to local councillors, MPs, departments of government and, in one instance, to Her Majesty the Queen.

The letters came from three of the prettiest corners of the kingdom. But they were not an orchestrated protest in search of something to complain about. They were specific, informed, concerned and compelling. They made their case.

The school, for example, is one of several village schools, housed in timber-framed 1960s buildings, that are threatened with closure because they were insubstantially built and have not been properly maintained since. And it has only 15 pupils.

The letter writer understands why the authorities want to close the school. But, as he goes on to say, the school, which is a first school, gives the children a first-rate and imaginative education, closely linked with the life around it.

It is, he says, the central pivot of the community. It provides a meeting ground for the adults as much as for the children.

He believes this is all the more important as rural life becomes more solitary. And his fear is that villages are easy to pick off, one by one. It is a fear shared by the inhabitants of an even smaller hamlet at the other end of the country.

On a green field site next to their village a developer wants to build an industrial chicken unit complete with a mobile home. It will, he says, create new job opportunities.

But there are only 26 adults in the village. Eighteen have

jobs in the hamlet itself, and the others have jobs nearby. And the chicken unit is not exactly labour intensive.

The villagers fear that the two huge galvanised poultry houses, plus the feed hopper and the mobile home, will be an eyesore. The traffic generated will be a menace on the narrow lanes and the place will probably smell. It will not offer much of a life for the chickens either, but that is another argument.

What distresses my correspondent is that if the chicken unit is built and prospers, it may develop into an agricultural industrial estate, and if it is built and fails it may be abandoned and become derelict.

If only, she said, the site had been protected.

Pause for hollow laughter from letter writer number three. His concern is for a proposal to build 40 executive houses on a piece of wasteland in a dock complex. Some time ago that piece of wasteland was designated a Site of Special Scientific Interest, an SSSI. It was so designated because both rare plants and rare butterflies are found there. The rarest plant on the site is the purple broomrape which is found nowhere else in the county and scarcely anywhere else in the country. The commonest plant on the site is kidney vetch on which the small blue butterfly feeds; the latter is a declining species throughout the land.

My correspondent's fear is that, if the development is allowed to go ahead, not only will that site be lost, but no other wildlife site in the county will be safe from the developers.

I have deliberately not identified the three locations, though you may already have deduced where at least one of them is.

What the three letters testify is that there is no substitute for local knowledge, for an intimate understanding of what really matters. One of the letter writers reminded me that I had once argued that most of the mistakes in, and on, the countryside are permitted, and committed, from ignorance.

To look after a place properly we need to know everything about it. Only then will we neither disfigure, diminish nor devalue the countryside.

The thundering juggernaut

❦ ❦ ❦

THE LAST TIME I was in the Yorkshire Dales I met a man who had seen a lorry stuck on a hump-backed bridge. Its wheels, front and rear, revolved helplessly, but those who witnessed this mishap were neither sympathetic nor helpful. Serves him right, they said, he cannot say that he had not been warned. And that is true. On the approach to that bridge, from both sides, there are official road signs which say "Beware of grounding", and they are accompanied by an illustration of a lorry stuck like a see-saw on the brow of the bridge. Such signs are common in the Dales where the roads are narrow and many bridges humped.

But signs alone do not deter the drivers who should not be there in the first place. If a road is not suitable for heavy lorries, they should not be using it. And in beautiful places it is no answer to say that the road must be "improved".

Whenever that conflict arises, the options are either wider roads or smaller vehicles. The former may be the answer on the trunk routes (which is why we built the motorways), but the latter is the only sensible answer in country places.

There are some villages in Britain now, especially in the south east of England, where juggernauts thunder through all day and every day. People are afraid to cross the village street, and even behind closed doors there is no escape from the noise.

The lorries are out of scale, out of place, out of order. No amount of pelican crossings, warning signs, or traffic signals can make amends. The heavy lorries should no more be there than locomotives from the main line or jumbo jets looking for an alternative to Gatwick.

The juggernauts make life intolerable. That is not to deny the importance of road transport. Ninety-nine per cent of everything that we eat and drink now travels by road. If there were no vehicles to transport it, the shelves of the shops and supermarkets would be empty.

The Road Lobby is right to complain that less of the Road Fund Licence money is spent on the roads in Britain than in other European countries. It is right to argue for the completion of the motorway network and for a higher standard of motorway construction.

There have to be trunk routes to carry both heavy traffic, which is a measure of volume, and heavy vehicles which are a measure of weight. It is where they go next that is the worry.

In a moment of madness it was once proposed that the main road through the Yorkshire Dales, the A684, should become a primary route, and signposted accordingly for traffic wishing to get from the A1 to the M6 and back again. Fortunately in that instance wiser heads prevailed.

But the folly continues. New sums are being done in Whitehall to seek to diminish on paper the impact of the heaviest vehicles. There is a new measurement called the passenger car unit, or pcu, and by that standard a car weighing say 3·8 tonnes has a value of 1 pcu whereas a lorry weighing 38 tonnes has a value of 2 pcus.

Pcu the other one, as they say.

It is one thing for a 38-tonne truck to travel up the M1, and pull into the Toddington service station; quite another for it to take a short cut through Toddington village to escape the jam on the motorway. It is too big for the village streets and ought not to be there. But who will deny it access?

We have speed limits on roads (not always obeyed) and we also have some (though not enough) weight limits. At the end of the lane in which I live there is a sign which indicates that lorries weighing more than 7·5 tonnes are not to use the lane, except for access. But who determines the right of access?

Not long ago when they thought they might strike oil in these parts, a seismic survey convoy weighing 90 tonnes announced that it intended to travel along our lane, which at one point is only 11 feet wide. Any damage, they said, would be minimal and compensated for. No thank you, the inhabitants of the lane replied as one voice, and with the help of our MP, the seismic convoy was repelled.

Anything over 7·5 tonnes is a menace. The milk tanker has to be admitted because it has a genuine need of access, but one heavy vehicle a day is quite enough and the tanker is a third of the weight of the heaviest road vehicles.

Sooner or later throughout the countryside those in authority will have to face up to this question. Are there not country roads where weight limits must not only be indicated but enforced, and where lorries over such and such a weight will not be allowed even for access? It ought to be as mandatory as a height restriction on a low bridge. There you have to turn back otherwise you slice the top off your vehicle. I once got a rented van stuck under a bridge outside a school on the day of the annual entrance examination. I had to let down the tyres and reverse swiftly in the face of angry parents convinced I was impeding their children's education.

Entrance to countless villages should be similarly impeded, not only with signs saying no through traffic over a given size, but no entry for whatever reason for anything else on wheels over a given size. And if that means that you will require two small removal vans instead of one large one when you move into or out of the village, so be it.

What is to be done, however, where the heavy vehicles are not visitors to the countryside but residents? Parish councillors in conference earlier this year were calling for greater control of heavy vehicles. They want the law changed so that they have a right to object to the grant of a licence to operate trucks. We know best the damage they can do locally, they say.

They could have quoted the statistic, which I read somewhere though do not wholly believe, that one 38-tonne truck does more damage to the road surface than 200,000 cars. True or not that seems another good reason for keeping 38-tonne trucks out of the Dales. Though it ought not to be used as an excuse to admit another 200,000 cars.

A hall for all

❦ ❦ ❦

EVERY VILLAGE SHOULD have:
a) a church*
b) a school*
c) a pub*
d) a post office*
e) a village hall*
*Delete whichever is inapplicable.

They sat with their pens poised.

Don't you dare cross out the village hall, said the large lady in the hat.

Why not? said the newcomer. We have a pub and a school. We can rent a room in one and the hall in the other.

Lucky you, said the large lady. Have you any idea how many villages have lost their schools, shops and surgeries?

In some villages the village hall is the only meeting place left. Some of them now house not only playgroups and adult classes, but are also the clinic, the sports hall and the post office.

She paused to confirm that she had their attention and then continued.

I went to a meeting in London last year, she said, and was appalled at what I learnt about the plight of village halls.

Did you know that in some counties the cost of business rates on village halls have gone up sixtyfold? And village halls are charities.

Did you know, she went on, that they are facing huge bills to update their kitchen and bathroom facilities and their fire alarm systems to meet the new regulations? I know it has to be done, but where will the money come from?

The retired businessman among us looked up with interest.

Where indeed? he said. It seems to me that we have to run our village halls as business-like charities. I gather that less than half can meet their running costs from hire charges, largely because they do not want to charge people too much. That's true, said the lady in the hat. A quarter of them do receive regular help from their parish council, but only half get full rate relief.

In that case, said the retired executive, it is up to us to campaign locally to make sure that our parish council and our district council and our county council do everything that they can to relieve our burdens. Best practice, I would call it.

And, said the lady in the hat, it is up to us, and our Member of Parliament, to make sure that the Government does everything in its power.

It is absurd, is it not, that we have to pay VAT not only on any extension or alteration to the village hall, but also on the fuel and power supplies?

The newcomer was not convinced.

I can see your point, she said, but I still do not understand why you think it is so important to have a village hall.

If you have a church and a school and a pub and a post office, you don't need one. And if you haven't, you probably don't want one.

Rubbish, said the retired gent, gently aroused. If you have none of the five, then your village is little more than a housing estate, however ancient.

And even if you have the other four, you have to remember (and at this point he looked at me) that not everybody goes to church, not everyone frequents the pub, and that most of us went to school a long time ago.

I could be silent no longer.

It seems to me, I said, that even if the church is full every Sunday, even if the school thrives, even if the pub is packed every evening, even if the post office is besieged, you still need a village hall.

Why? said the newcomer.

Because, I said, it is the community's own assembly hall, in which the people can come together for any purpose they choose. It is not a rival to the other four, but an addition. It enriches the community.

If it is computerised, said a young man in the corner. He had not spoken previously, largely because he had a headset clamped to his skull.

In my village, he said, we have the first telecottage in England.

Tele . . . what? said a chorus.

Telecottage. It is housed in the village primary school. It was funded by the county council and the Rural Development Commission. It has three computers, a TV teletext facility, a fax machine, a laser printer, everything.

It functions as a training centre, a library, an electronic post office, a data processing services bureau, a communications workshop and a teleshop. It is a meeting place where neighbours get together for a chat or drop in to use the equipment.

Who drops in? said the newcomer.

Well, said the young man, it is used by community groups such as the parish council, the Women's Institute, youth organisations, playgroups, farmers, businessmen, people working from home – plus, of course, the children in the primary school.

Then I remembered where it is, on the Staffordshire Moorlands.

I drive through your village every week, I said. I love the church.

Learn to love the telecottage, he said. It is the village hall of the future.

Bobby on the beat

❦ ❦ ❦

THE LOLLIPOP LADY stepped out into the road, presented arms, and signalled me to stop. I pulled up obediently.

With a wave of her right hand, she then indicated to a group of young children gathered outside the school gate that it was now safe for them to cross the road. So they did, running off cheerfully with much merriment.

A man whom I took to be the caretaker closed the school gate, and I waited for the lollipop lady, her job now done, to wave me on. But instead she came up to the car.

I wound down the window.

I want a word with you, she said, and invited me to park in a reserved space just beyond the school. I did as she instructed, wondering what I had done wrong. I got out of the car and she came up to me.

I know who you are, she said, and I like what you write, but whenever you list what a village needs you always leave something and someone out.

Explain, I said.

Well, she replied, you say a village needs a church and a vicar, a pub and a publican, a school and a head teacher, a post office and a post mistress, and a village hall, but why do you always omit a police house and a village bobby?

Why do you ask? I said.

Because, she replied, we are about to lose ours.

And she went on to explain that in her part of the country many village policemen, occupying village police houses and working from them, are to be replaced by teams of policemen operating from the nearest town.

The authorities argue, she said, that the traditional village bobby is a romantic ideal of the past. They say that research shows that nowadays the village bobby deals with only a fraction of the incidents on his patch. Officers from the neighbouring communities take over whenever he is off duty.

They also argue that because the crime rate in rural areas is low they can make better use of the officers. There is no question of employing fewer officers but simply of reorganising their work.

And that, she said, is a nonsense. She knows for a fact that when village bobbies are drafted into town forces, they do less and less proper police work and more and more report writing. They call it "paralysis by analysis", she said.

The crime rate is low in her village precisely because the village policeman is there all the time. He is the deterrent. He is working even when officially off duty. People call at or ring up the police house to discuss their problems. Even in the village pub he picks up useful information.

It is social work, she said, community work, and the village bobby has to be part of the village community to carry out his work properly.

She has a friend who is married to a village bobby who is about to be transferred to the nearest town. His predecessor served in the same village for 25 years and is now referred to as "the last great village policeman".

Her friend's husband had hoped to emulate him, to become part of the community. Now he fears, and the villagers fear, that his local knowledge will be dissipated.

And his wife fears that she may have to give up her job because he will need their car to get to work every day. They might even lose their police house in the village.

But our real worry here, said the lollipop lady, is that crime will increase. The local farmers say that their tools and their equipment, their vehicles and their livestock, are all targets for thieves from the cities.

We have a Farmwatch scheme whereby the farmers inform the police of any suspicious activity, but we still want to keep our Country Beat officer, our village bobby, who works from the village police house and is here all of the time.

She reached into her raincoat pocket and showed me a copy of a letter from the Clerk of the Parish Council to the Chief Constable.

It called for the continuation of the old tried, tested and proven method of working. The close contact between the village constable and the parishioners, it said, resulted in very low crime levels, a good flow of vital information, the swift apprehension of criminals, and prompt attention to all matters requiring police attention.

That says it all, she said.

At that moment a police car drove up and a police officer got out. He is going to do me for parking in a reserved space, I thought.

But he walked straight past me and kissed the lollipop lady.

This, she said by way of explanation, is my husband.

3

High
in the
Sky

Make hay when the sun shines

❦ ❦ ❦

THERE WAS A time, Wordsworth said, when every meadow appeared to him apparelled, as he put it, in celestial light. But not for long. The things which I have seen, he wrote, I now can see no more. He blamed himself, and the loss of the innocence of youth. Today he would be hard pressed to find a meadow to moon over.

Many meadows disappeared during the Second World War when we were digging for victory. (It worked; we won.) Many more meadows – 95 per cent in all – have disappeared since the war, either under the plough or under the fertiliser. A meadow is more than a field of grass. It is usually defined as grassland mown for hay, as distinct from pasture which is grassland grazed by animals.

But a meadow is more than a hayfield. It is a hayfield having a hard time. Meadows thrive on stress. They like what is now called "a stressed environment", where everything fights for survival on equal terms, not "an improved environment", where fertiliser favours the few and reduces the number of species that will grow.

And a meadow is not out of bounds. Little Boy Blue under the haystack fast asleep was ticked off because there were sheep in the meadow and cows in the corn. Cows are welcome in the meadow after the hay has been cut, but sheep never. They nibble far too close to the ground.

So meadows need managing, looking after, but that is not the same as surrounding them with signs saying Keep Out. They are the products of use, of mowing and of grazing.

Farmers used to reckon that it took about 150 years to make a really good meadow, which is why they looked upon them as investments. They valued them for the hay and the pasture, but they also valued them as the heart of the countryside.

They were rich both in grasses and in wild flowers. Meadow cranesbill and mouse-ear, betony and lady's bedstraw, sweet vernal grass and Yorkshire-fog, black medick and yellow rattle.

They were rich, too, in wildlife. Not only butterflies and moths, ants and other insects, but the small animals and birds which preyed upon them; moles and voles, shrews and bats. The barn owl is faced with extinction precisely because there are so few meadows where it can hunt for fresh meat.

And human beings themselves have lost something with the disappearance of the meadows. Where else can they make hay when the sun shines?

That, of course, is the dilemma. Haymaking is hazardous, too dependent on the weather. It is more efficient and economic to grow grass for silage, cutting it earlier in the year when it is green and wet, before the seedheads drop.

You might even get two crops a year if you apply plenty of fertiliser, but in the process you will have encouraged the grass to grow and discouraged everything else. What was once a meadow will now be a silage factory.

All, however, is not lost. Farmers are once again being encouraged to let the flowers grow. Flower-rich meadows can now qualify as Environmentally Sensitive Areas (ESAs). Keep it like that, says the Ministry, and we shall pay you.

And although meadows take a long time to mature, there is a growing do-it-yourself market in meadow making. It is the opposite to the creation of a virgin lawn. To grow your own meadow, you must first neglect the soil. Feed it neither with fertiliser nor with compost, and if it seems too rich scrape off the topsoil.

Then in late summer sow it with seed – native seeds of grasses and flowers. It is no use importing fritillaries raised in hot houses in Holland and expecting them to flourish. And avoid any seed mixture that includes rye grass because it will not mix with flowers.

But there are many excellent seed mixes now. There is the RSPB mix and the BTCV mix, and even the BBC Wildlife mix. Sow that one, I was told, and you get TV producers from BBC Bristol crawling through your undergrowth.

Whatever you sow, mix it with sand, so it is not sown too thickly. And be patient. The grasses should germinate quickly but the flowers will take a little longer. Cowslips, for instance, are particularly stubborn and may not make an appearance until there have been two or three hard winters.

I tried my hand at this a few years ago, or more accurately my wife did, and the result was a treat. We left the mowing late and we are wiser now. But then we are spoiled. Up the lane where we live is a meadow that a farmer and his family before him have treasured for generations. It is like a slice of history. Wordsworth would have loved it. Remember what he said: "Earth fills her lap with pleasures of her own."

Why animals don't have wheels

<SCARCELY anyone>, or so I used to believe, has a kind word for snails. Even Dougal in *The Magic Roundabout*, who was kind to everyone, put down Brian the Snail with the magisterial rebuke: Don't push your luck, little mollusc.

Serve him right, I thought. But I was wrong. I blame the generation gap. When I was at school we could study Latin and Greek, history and geography, physics and chemistry, but nothing biological. Perhaps they thought it would give us ideas.

So, over the years I have had to rely on chance encounters, *Wildlife on One* and the wisdom of my children to learn about Nature. It helps to have a son who teaches zoology and who once gave a course of lectures entitled "Why Animals Don't Have Wheels". Not to mention a daughter-in-law who studies competitive genes in pollen.

Indeed, most of the young people I meet seem to be encyclopaedic about natural history, which explains the current enthusiasm for conservation. It is not fashion, but knowledge. And snails, I have discovered, have a lot to teach us.

It was when I was describing the contents of a garden pond and failed to make any mention of the snails that I was made aware of the gap in my education. Did you never, I was asked, organise a snail race at school? I confessed I never had and enquired how long a snail took to complete a race. It depended how long we had, came the reply. But we preferred watching them mate. I thought they were hermaphrodite creatures, both sexes at the same time, self-contained, I said. Yes, a single individual snail can produce both male and female sex cells, but before the eggs of any one snail can develop they must be fertilised by the sperm of another, while both are in the temporary male phase. You can see them on warm, damp summer evenings. They circle each other and then fire sperm darts at each other. Fascinating.

After that there was nothing for it but to sit down with a

book on snails, from which I learned that snails have been around a long time, longer than us. They are cold-blooded creatures with no means of regulating their temperatures. They can withdraw into their shells and secrete a temporary waterproof lid over the shell mouth. But they cannot leave home. Their bodies are fastened to their shells as our muscles are to our bones. Their shells grow as their bodies grow, and the whorls turn clockwise. If you find an anticlockwise one it is a collector's piece.

A snail can stick its head and its foot out of doors, but the rest of it never leaves the shell. Its foot is like no other. It is simply something muscular to move with, and it moves on its own thin ribbon of excreted mucus. It may move slowly but it moves safely. On its mucus trail it can glide over even the sharp edge of a razor without getting cut.

It will eat lettuce and strawberries and soft seedlings, but it is just as happy feeding on garden rubbish and weeds. And it has no fewer than 14,000 teeth. Its eyes are on the end of its tentacles, the longer, posterior pair, but it is near-sighted, and it can pull in its tentacles like the fingers of a glove.

Snails may not be part of the enterprise economy but they are economically significant. They may destroy some crops but they also provide food for man and for the food organisms, such as fish, that man eats. Thrushes feed on them. So do hedgehogs and mice and shrews. Beetles and glow-worms eat them and so do 65 different species of flies in Britain.

All that they can cope with. But man is a problem. Almost everything he does makes their lives difficult or impossible. He destroys their habitats or poisons them. He pollutes their water, fouls their air and burns their grassland.

No one summons an international conference to Save the Snail, and yet everything it has to put up with is as much a threat to the species as the hole in the ozone layer or the greenhouse effect is to us. A snail is a very sensitive creature. We should look after it, in its interest and in our own.

As Brian the Snail would put it; Don't push your luck, little biped.

Free, flexible and creative
❦ ❦ ❦

"IT IS THE great peril of our society," wrote G K Chesterton, "that all its mechanism may grow more fixed while its spirit grows more fickle. A man's minor actions and arrangements ought to be free, flexible, creative; the things that should be unchangeable are his principles, his ideals." And when asked to explain what he meant, Chesterton replied: "A man can get used to getting up at five o'clock in the morning. A man cannot very well get used to being burnt for his opinions; the first experiment is commonly fatal." For the past 15 years I have been getting up before five o'clock in the morning (at 4.32am to be precise), three or four days a week, and it is no hardship. Kind souls have sought to commiserate with me, but in truth the world is a nicer place at that hour. The tumult and the conflict which characterise city life at high noon are absent, and I can even hear birdsong in the Barbican.

In the country it is better still. When I was first invited to be a morning broadcaster I hesitated precisely because it meant rising so early. Then I met a gamekeeper in the Lake District who in summer regularly rises at 2.30am. It is the only time, he said, when you see the world as it is meant to be.

Dorothy Wordsworth would have agreed with him. Day begins at dawn in entry after entry in her Grasmere Journal, and her brother William was at his desk as soon as there was sufficient light to see to write.

Most writers like an early start, though not all bless the dawn. There are more grey dawns than dappled dawns in English poetry, but almost all affirm that morning is the time to be creative. New every morning, as the hymn writer says. And yet over the centuries people have had very different views of when day begins. The ancient Greeks and the ancient Britons thought day began at sunset, which is why we call two weeks a fortnight and not a fortday.

The Babylonians and the Persians, on the other hand, thought day began at sunrise, but the ancient Egyptians (and for that matter modern astronomers) said day began at noon. Whereas we, like the Romans, date the start of the day at midnight.

Only on election nights do I broadcast at that hour and I never know whether to say: "It is midnight on Thursday," or "It is midnight on Friday." So I always say simply: "It is midnight." And then when we finish – usually around three o'clock – I am in two minds whether to say Good night or Good morning.

I remember when Alistair Cooke was given the freedom of the City of Manchester there was a banquet in his honour in the Town Hall, and so many people spoke in tribute to him that when he rose to his feet it had turned midnight. "This," he said, "is the first time I have made an after-dinner speech in dawn's early light."

That early light shows the night worker the way to bed. When I worked on a morning newspaper I turned in at the hour at which I now get up. And you can get used to both. But I think we are not naturally nocturnal creatures. Given the choice I would settle for day work, not night work, and an early start.

I would also settle for Greenwich Mean Time, all year round. It seems absurd to sit astride the meridian of Greenwich and then to monkey about with the clock. Daylight saving, the idea of making fuller use of daylight by advancing the clock an hour in the summer months instead of simply getting up an hour earlier, seems silly to me. It was first adopted by the Germans as a wartime measure in 1916 and we followed hastily.

Between the wars, we had British Summer Time in the summer months only, but in the Second World War we had British Summer Time in the winter months and Double Summer Time in summer. It was light, I remember, almost until midnight in midsummer, but of course the real time was 10 o'clock.

After the war we reverted to Summer Time in the summer months only, save for the summer of 1947 when there was a need to save fuel and we had Double Summer Time.

Then in February 1968 the clocks were advanced one hour and we were told that there would be no going back. British Summer Time was from then on to be British Standard Time, year in and year out.

It did not work. It was too dark in the winter mornings. No matter what the clock said the cows knew it was too early to be milked. So the next October the clocks went back.

Now there is talk of Britain falling in step with Europe and having either the wartime regime of Summer Time and Double Summer Time, or British Standard Time the year round.

Nonsense.

What we need is not British Standard Time, but Standard Time, the system of time-keeping accepted in most parts of the world. Standard Time is the sun's time, and when it is noon over Greenwich it should be noon over Britain, all the year round.

If the hour is inconvenient we should change the timetable not the time. Get up an hour earlier in summer, or an hour later in winter. Be free, flexible and creative in our minor arrangements, as Chesterton said.

He stuck to his principles and stayed in bed until he was ready to get up. When asked why, he replied: "Misers get up early in the morning; and burglars, I am informed, get up the night before."

Where feet may safely tread

❧ ❧ ❧

ONE FINE SUMMER Sunday two out of every five people in Britain venture into the countryside, and most of them go for a walk. Two out of every five is roughly 18 million and, as most of them have two legs, that is a lot of feet.

When I lived halfway up Helvellyn I would hear them trampling past the door striding towards Striding Edge, where they would queue to cross like pedestrians at a pelican crossing. Wherever walkers choose to congregate – on the summit of Snowdon, at the southern end of the Pennine Way, on the Three Peaks in the Yorkshire Dales, on Ivinghoe Beacon – their footsteps wear away the paths.

There is even talk of laying a plastic carpet in the Dales, and it has been suggested that some favourite paths may have to be closed for a while to give them time to recover. But that, in itself, is not the answer. It is not restricted access we need, but wider access. Not fewer people, but more paths.

It is said that 84 per cent of the population visit the countryside at least once a year, and 88 per cent would not dream of following a path that is not clearly marked. I blame Sunday School: it is the fear of being guilty of trespass, a word which suggests not merely an offence but a sin. And yet there are no fewer than 100,000 miles of country paths where the public has legitimate rights of way. Why are so many of those miles not our chosen paths? Why do so many people return over and over again to the same place?

The obvious answer is because they like it and they enjoy seeing it change over the seasons and they want to remember how it looked this time last year. But they also return to it because they are not sure where else to go. A path was originally something more than the shortest convenient route from A to B; it was the most interesting convenient route from A to B. It followed the intimate pattern of the countryside – the hedgerows, the stepping stones, the corners of the field – with occasional diversions to take in anything of interest: a pond perhaps, or a blasted oak.

It was both a route and a journey, which was why country people got very cross when landowners attempted to close public paths. It was no comfort to them that there was an alternative route which might or might not be no greater distance. It was their choice that was being restricted, not just their access.

Since 1949, local authorities have had to record all public paths in their areas and publish the information in footpath maps. They are also responsible for making sure that the paths are clearly signposted and unobstructed. And the public is at liberty to remove any obstruction. It is, however, one thing to protect the route, quite another to preserve the journey. A path through a meadow loses most of its appeal if the meadow is built upon. The right of way remains intact, but who wants to exercise that right other than a man from the new housing estate exercising his dog?

And in the countryside proper the great threat to the public path has been the removal of field boundaries to make way for intensive farming. The landmarks that signalled not only the routes of a path but its very reason have gone – the hedgerows, the ponds, the coppices.

The paths still remain, often more clearly signposted than before, "Public Footpath," the sign proclaims, but who wants to walk across a huge featureless field? Especially as the path can be ploughed up or sown as long as it is subsequently reinstated, which can take time. But intensive farming produced unsold and unsellable surpluses, and now that land has been taken out of production there is a great opportunity to make the most of our footpaths. Perhaps we should call it a Pathfinder Campaign.

We must begin with the best and journey on. Not all public paths pass through countryside where most of the wildlife habitat or the landscape interest has been destroyed. There are still many miles of paths where we can enjoy the wildlife, the landscape, and the view.

These we must enhance, using the right of way as the justification for planting trees and hedgerows, sowing wildflowers, restoring the grassy banks, until every path becomes recognisably a country lane again.

And where paths lead to land which has been taken out of intensive produciton, these released parcels should be managed as new habitats for wildlife or as quiet corners for people to enjoy.

Above all people need to know where they may safely tread. It is a parish matter and each (as some already do) should publish a simple guide to its public paths, available at every village shop and pub and filling station, so that people heading for the already overcrowded paths may turn aside with thanksgiving.

While there are places where it is fair to say that too many feet walk upon England's mountains green, there will not be too many if we enhance the network of public paths throughout the countryside and press for access to wander at will over open land or mountain and moor.

Then on any fine summer Sunday we shall all be free to go for a walk in the country without doing any damage or getting in each other's way.

Buckets and spades

❦ ❦ ❦

IN A CITY supermarket I overheard this exchange between two women in the queue, each of whom had a loaded trolley topped with a small child.

Are you going to the seaside for your summer holiday? asked one.

No, replied the other, we are going to the country.

The distinction stirred old memories, and not only because neither had mentioned the Costa del Somewhere. Clearly both were taking their holidays at home this year, meaning away but not abroad.

That is how it used to be. In the schoolyard at our elementary school, in the years before the Second World War, no one had heard of Marbella or Majorca and no one was rich enough to visit Monte Carlo or Biarritz. But nonetheless there was one distinct preference – the coast rather than the country.

The summer holiday meant going to the seaside with a bucket and spade; anything else was inadequate. Even those who could boast that they were going to stay on a farm were thought to have missed out. The beach was the place to be, especially in August.

There was, as I recall, no mention of pollution, though sewers then as now no doubt emptied into the sea. Nor were there any complaints about overcrowding, for how else could you build the biggest and the best sandcastle on the beach unless there was competition?

The excitement of arriving at the seafront was second only to opening your eyes on Christmas morning as the best moment of the year. To reach the edge of the cliff or even the rail along the promenade and to see the sea was better than any present.

It mattered not how often you went to the seaside, and

we lived not many miles from the sea. It mattered not whether you came to a quiet spot on the coast or to a busy resort, and in Northumberland we were spoiled for choice. What mattered was that you were beside the sea, *and* on the beach where shingle was no substitute for sand.

Mothers fussed about the windbreak and about sand in the sandwiches. Fathers complained about the cost of ice-creams. Older sisters postured like pin-ups, and older brothers practised their press-ups. But little ones were oblivious to all that, lost in the delights of sea and sand.

Looking back I suspect that a holiday by the sea is the first real taste of freedom unconstrained by the garden fence or the playground wall. The sea stretches to the horizon and the world seems limitless.

I made this point at a conference on the protection of the coastline and was clearly thought to be dotty, if harmless. Much had been made of the threat to wildlife, with which I agreed, and to the dangers of pollution as they affect all species, including us. But nobody else seemed very concerned about the sheer delight of the seashore. They knew all the planning designations (so did I). They knew all the EEC regulations (they had me there). But they had forgotten the magic.

A single bloom, a singing bird, a wisp of cloud, a setting sun – all these are wonders of creation which make you pause and reflect. But is not the coast, the place where land and sea meet, special?

I know there is a lot of it and if you live on an island it is easily accessible, but familiarity should not make us forgetful. The combination of greed and neglect which has fouled so much of our coastline is a national disgrace, but it is not enough to argue the case for conservation without remembering why.

At that conference the argument developed into a clash of acronyms and acrimony, and when one chap spoke up for the seaside resorts they fell upon him like seagulls on sewage.

I rose in his defence. He had argued that even in

Blackpool, where nothing succeeds like excess, it was always a joy to walk along the beach in the early morning or the early evening when the tide was out.

I pointed out that that is true, and that the less succesful resorts need encouragement too, not to make themselves vulgar and brash, but prosperous and busy.

A decaying resort is no good to anyone, and we need the contrast between the well-kept seaside town with a busy seafront and a bustling harbour, and the unspoiled coastal tract where only the walkers wander and the wildlife grows.

Inland we would call it the distinction between town and country. On the coast the distinction is all the more valid. There should be nothing nasty by the sea. But it cannot all be remote.

The poet said he would go down to the sea again, to the lonely sea and the sky. But he cannot expect to have it to himself, not all of it.

So in addition to the long-overdue campaign to protect the British coastline and to clean up the beaches and the sea, I think we should begin work on restoring the resorts.

Many are beautiful places in themselves – Whitby and Scarborough, Llandudno and Tenby, almost any towns that you can think of – and all of them putting their best faces towards the sea.

They each have an architecture of their own which ought not to be defiled by the kind of accretions which have disfigured the Mediterranean coast.

They should be made conservation areas in their own right, lovingly restored, kept to scale, happily occupied. Then we can all go down to the seaside – those with the buckets and spades first.

One man went to mow
❦ ❦ ❦

"NOTHING," WROTE Francis Bacon at the end of the 16th century, "is more pleasant to the eye than green grass finely shorn." And he was right. Not, I imagine, that he ever mowed his own lawn; gentlemen seldom did.

But the British have always been good at grass. In the 18th century a Frenchman, d'Argenville, wrote: "You can't do better than to follow the method of cultivation used in England, where their grass plots are so exquisite a beauty, that in France we can scarce ever hope to come up to it." And that is still true.

And a German, von Archenholz, wrote: "The grass in England is of incomparable beauty . . . often so level, they can play at bowls upon it as on a billiard table."

Everyone claims to know why. Climate and geology make it so. They give us, said one early English chronicler, "turf thick yset, and soft as any velvet". But he, like all the others, failed to make any mention of the maintenance.

It was a gardener at one of the oldest colleges in Cambridge who is credited with the ultimate explanation of the beauty of the British lawn. Asked by a visiting American why the lawn was in such excellent condition, he replied: "It is very simple, Sir. It has been mowed and rolled every day for four hundred years." Though even he failed to add that Fellows of the College alone are allowed to tread upon it. Everyone else must keep off the grass. And he made no mention of Mr Budding.

Mr Budding is the man who invented the lawnmower. It is true that a Mr Plucknett (yes, Plucknett not Plunkett) patented a machine for mowing corn and grass in 1805 but it appears not to have caught on.

In 1830 Edwin Beard Budding, of Stroud in Gloucestershire, signed articles of agreement with John

Ferrabee covering the finances required to make a machine for "cropping or shearing the vegetable surface of lawns, grass plots or pleasure grounds". The patent for his "machine for mowing lawns" is dated 31 August, 1830. We should call it Budding Day.

Mr Budding has never been given his due. Half the gardening reference books get his first name wrong. They call him Edward, not Edwin. And no one, as far as I know, has thought to erect a statue to him. And yet, think what we owe to this man.

His original 19-inch roller mower looked very like a modern mower except that the collecting box resembled a seed tray. It used the principle of rotating cutters operating against a fixed cutter, which was an idea he adapted from the method of shearing nap from cloth, employed in the textile mill where Budding had worked as an engineer.

Ransome's of Ipswich agreed to begin manufacturing Budding's machine in 1832, although at first it seems to have been thought of more as a rich man's toy than an everyday implement. "Country gentlemen," Budding said, "may find in using my machine themselves an amusing, useful and healthy exercise."

And in 1840, in her famous book *Instructions in Gardening for Ladies*, Mrs Jane Loudon said that frequent mowing of the lawn was an operation "which a lady cannot very well perform for herself; unless indeed she have strength enough to use one of Budding's mowing machines".

A year later, in her *Ladies' Companion to the Flower Garden*, Mrs Loudon was still wary: "A substitute for mowing with the scythe has lately been introduced in the form of the mowing-machine . . . It is particularly adapted for amateurs, affording an excellent exercise to the arms and every part of the body; but it is proper to observe that many gardeners are prejudiced against it."

That prejudice was soon overcome. By the 1870s in

Beeton's *Dictionary of Gardening* the lawnmower was acknowledged. "Their use is too well known to need description. . . . These useful machines are fast supplanting the scythe both on large and small lawns."

The invention of the lawnmower not only encouraged the spread of the suburban garden, but also determined what kind of garden it would be. Any householder with a bit of land alongside his house can plant flowers and vegetables. But that is a cottage garden.

By putting a neat and tidy lawn within everyone's grasp, the lawnmower has made possible the return of the formal garden – the garden of the country house, albeit on a much smaller scale. And the mowing has got easier.

Ransome's added side wheels in 1869, and after that came the motor mower, the electric mower, the hover mower.

You can walk behind or sit astride your machine. You can even have a remote-controlled mower and operate it from a deckchair. But that is no posture for a Budding gardener.

Suburban summer

❦ ❦ ❦

AUGUST IS NOT well thought-of. The Saxons called it weed-month because everything was overgrown. The French Revolutionaries called it Thermidor because everywhere was too hot. And today travel agents try to talk you out of going on holiday during it – as if most people have any choice. August *is* the holiday month.

Holidaymaking has a happy ring; tourism sounds like a threat. One is a pursuit; the other a trade. But it is an essential trade, the best redistributor of wealth since the invention of taxation.

Compiling a catalogue of the virtues of tourism, I very quickly hit upon a substantial list. Tourism brings in money. Visitors arrive intending to spend. It creates jobs and checks depopulation. It inspires the preservation and the improvement of the good things of the past. It prompts the development of better services, facilities and amenities for visitors and inhabitants alike. It can enrich the environment, and it can restore pride in places.

But without planning and control, it can create over-crowding and congestion, pollution and noise, erosion and squalor, vandalism and litter. I thereupon coined the couplet:

Tourism can spoil or it can enhance,

But it cannot be left to chance.

This is especially so in the English countryside, where scale is everything, and one careless clumsy development can ruin a whole landscape. And yet more and more people want to have a holiday in the country, so how can they all be accommodated without over-running the place? The Peak National Park published a survey of its visitors a few years ago. It discovered that there are more than 18 million visits in a year. Over 95 per cent of the people who come have been before. Five million people come regularly but mostly on day trips. Only 10 per cent of the visitors stay overnight, and 80 per cent of their holidays last for fewer than seven days.

In the summer, over half the visitors staying there are on camping or caravanning holidays. And nearly half the visitors on holiday stay in the towns and villages which surround the Park, rather than in it.

What they appreciate most is the unspoiled landscape, the wildlife, and the *uncommercialised* nature of the Peaks. That, they said when asked, is very important. And so it is. The country has to have an income and has to provide work. With so few people now employed in agriculture, tourism is not only welcome, it is essential.

And there are many appropriate ways of holidaying in the country. You can stay in a farm, rent a cottage, lodge in a hostel, hire a caravan on a well-run site, or, if you can afford it, luxuriate in a country-house hotel.

All this is to be encouraged. It is tourism demonstrating that it is good for the economy and good for the environment and, most important of all, good for people. It makes them happy. But as demand increases it is going to take great ingenuity to expand the accommodation without converting the country into an extension of the suburbs.

Swaledale, for instance, has the finest collection of unwanted stone barns in Britain; unwanted in the sense of being of no further use to the farms, but very much wanted in the sense that they, and the dry-stone walls which surround them, are now a recognised essential feature of the landscape.

They are falling into ruin to such an extent that everyone concerned – the National Park, the Countryside Commission, English Heritage, the Ministry of Agriculture, the National Farmers' Union and the Country Landowners Association – have got together to devise a scheme to pay the farmers to rehabilitate the barns.

But for what purpose? They will look better but will they have a use? A start has been made on the bunkhouse barn project – the conversion of disused barns for the accommodation of holidaymakers; "stone tents" as some people have started calling them.

Can that be extended? Is it possible to accommodate people in small barns without a great extension of services – electricity, water, sewerage? Will visitors insist on driving right up to a barn? Or can some provision of simple comfort be achieved without turning every barn into a baby bungalow with a stone gnome on the step and a TV aerial on the roof?

I believe it can. What we need is the intelligent conversion of unwanted farm buildings into tourist accommodation that will be of the country and not imposed upon the country. There is no better way to spend a week or a weekend than in the English countryside – even in August.

4

Harvest
to
Hallowe'en

In pursuit of production

❦ ❦ ❦

A LONG TIME ago, in 1941, I spent my summer holidays on a farm. It was not difficult to arrange because I went to stay with the same farmer with whom I had spent the whole of the previous year as an evacuee.

But he and his wife had moved. In 1939 when I arrived with my gas mask from Newcastle they lived in a farm in the grounds of a castle in what was then called Cumberland (and still should be). It was a small farm. They had hens and ducks of their own, but as tenants of the family in the big house they were commissioned to rear only beef cattle. However, for me it was heaven on earth.

I went to bed by candlelight, slept on a feather mattress, collected the eggs, and was even allowed, in the company of Spot the dog, to drive cattle to market. Spot knew the way. It was like a nursery rhyme come true.

But then The Scholarship, as we called the 11-plus, intervened. I was dispatched to the grammar school, which itself had been evacuated from the big city to a small town. That too was a heady experience, but I still hankered for the farm life.

And so it came to pass that when we broke up for the summer holidays in 1941, I set off on my bike to the farmer's new settlement. It was, incidentally, a journey of about 20 miles, and it is an interesting reflection on the times that no one saw any danger in an 11-year-old embarking on such a trip alone.

The new farm was majestic — a handsome house, a huge acreage, a dairy herd as well as beef cattle, sheep as well as shire horses, and no tractor. It must have been a long summer holiday because I managed to be there both for the haymaking and the harvest.

I returned to school in mid-September firmly persuaded that farming was the essential life of the countryside. And all these years later I remain convinced of this.

When I first became involved in what I suppose can be called the politics of conservation, I was swift to argue that farmers are the essential inhabitants of the countryside, and not least of the most beautiful parts of the countryside. It is they who have shaped the landscapes we all love.

But there is much more to farming than that. John Dower, the father of the National Parks, got it right when he said that we look to the farming communities for the continuance not only of the landscape but of the drama itself, rural life and work. He was much given to quoting that wonderful phrase to describe the endless battle between man and nature: "the mild continuous epic of the soil".

It is a phrase that I think ought to be recited wherever people meet to discuss the future of farming, and recited with special emphasis on the words "mild" and "continuous". There has been too much upheaval, too much conflict, too much misunderstanding, about farming and the countryside.

The Prince of Wales put his finger on it when he said that the crisis in farming is a cultural crisis. It concerns the very identity of farming. Farming is not just another business. It is not like any other business. It is, or it should be, a special way of life. And he called it the long-term stewardship of a precious natural resource. He also pointed out that although the new technology of agriculture is here to stay, we need to retrieve the wisdom of the past.

The catalogue of recent error is now common knowledge. We all know, and indeed can see with our own eyes, the damage that has been done to the countryside in pursuit of production.

That is the direct result of treating farming as if it were simply another business. It was thought to be efficient to increase the yield to produce more than we need at a price which is more than we can pay and then dump the surplus on the world market, leaving the farmer with nothing. Nor is it sensible to flee from farming and treat farmers as if they were simply game-wardens or wood-rangers or park-keepers.

The farmers' calling is more than a livelihood, it is a way of life. Their land is more than an address, it is a territory. They belong to the countryside and were they to be evicted the countryside itself would cease to exist.

They need to farm, and the countryside needs to be farmed. As it always has been. It is the tradition. But a return to traditional farming does not mean wearing smocks again or having only three little pigs. It means having a respect for the past, concern for the present, and an eye to the future.

A tradition is not a matter of being set in your ways. It is a flow of sympathy, a sustained endeavour, a careful husbandry. I already knew the right word for it when I was 11.

Farming.

Sow and reap
❧ ❧ ❧

HARVEST TIME IS not what it was. It is not even when it was. We still celebrate it to coincide with the harvest moon, the full moon nearest the autumn equinox, which rises for several days at about sunset and gives a longer run of moonlit evenings than is usual, but the crops have been gathered long before.

By the time the vicar's wife is organising the harvest festival, next year's early crops have already been sown, which helps to explain why small boys are often reduced to taking tins of sardines to church as their contribution to the gathering. Though I suppose it is acceptable if they do it with a smile for, as Paul said to the Corinthians, God loves a cheerful giver.

A friend of mine swears that she once took a lump of coal to her school's harvest thanksgiving, quoting first Psalm 67 – The land has yielded its harvest – and then arguing successfully that this was a fruit of the earth (Psalm 104). It was a church school.

But I miss the real thing. I remember the summer and autumn of 1940 not because of what was happening in the war but because of what was happening in the fields. I saw for the first time in my life the corn cut, the stooks stacked, the rabbits run. I was allowed to take the men their elevenses and their tea, but I was too young to attend the harvest supper, though I heard the revelry of those returning.

In those days the farm calendar was in step with the seasons. Ploughing, sowing, reaping, and giving thanks had their fixed times in the year which even the weather could not divert by more than a week or two. The harvest was both the product and the reward for the year's work.

A combination of chemistry, subsidy, and sophistry has changed all that. The harvest is not only earlier, it is more frequent. Lately it has been an embarrassment too, as the grain mountains testify. Curious crops, like oilseed rape, have erupted all over the place turning the countryside an alien yellow.

Bees like oilseed rape and, although it is drenched in chemicals, it still relies on them first for pollination. Farmers have therefore taken to inviting beekeepers to bring their hives on to the rape fields early in the year. The bees work and then the farmers spray – and sometimes kill the bees, which seems a touch ungrateful. Fortunately for the bees, and for the rest of us, the subsidies for oilseed rape are now being reduced.

It is now accepted that intensive cultivation has been overdone, so farmers are encouraged to diversify. It may not be a return to the old days but it will be an improvement.

Many activities on the farm are subsidised. They include the creation of farm shops, of pick-your-own fruit sites, of camping and caravan sites, of tea rooms and restaurants, of squash and tennis courts. Farmers are encouraged to provide football pitches and water-sports sites, pitch-and-putt courses and play areas, picnic sites and farm museums, and ponds for angling.

Under the Farm Woodlands Scheme farmers are paid to plant trees to reduce output on improved agricultural land with higher grants for broadleaved planting to discourage the conifer. There should be grants too for the management of existing deciduous woods on the uplands.

It could, of course, all get out of hand with farms turned into trading estates and car parks everywhere. What is necessary is to make all farming and forestry development subject to planning laws to maintain a sense of proportion.

For 20 years farmers were paid to do the wrong thing. Now some of them are paid to do the right things to provide them with a decent living without disfiguring the countryside.

It is all a matter of scale. Agricultural policy in the Eighties was wrong because it was concerned only with volume, with quantity not quality. A farmhouse product is not meant to be mass produced. It should be distinctive, local, treasured.

If we get it right we shall be able to restore the real meaning to harvest thanksgiving, a celebration of the hereabouts, of the husbandry, the craft, the garnering, and the devotion.

The hedgehog hotline

I HAVE NEVER been on speaking terms with a hedgehog. I have addressed moles, flattered ferrets, and conversed with cats for hours on end, but I have never exchanged a word either of greeting or of rebuke with a hedgehog.

I have seldom run into one, and mercifully have never run over one, though I have seen far too many dead by the roadside. I began to think that I would never get to know about one, let alone get to know one, when one morning I had to introduce a report on the radio about Hogline.

Hogline was a hotline set up by the Avon Wildlife Trust to bring to the attention of the public the plight of the hedgehog. And the public was agog. People, it appears, do not know how to care for hedgehogs. So they asked. One woman in West Sussex wrote to me and said: "How do you keep a hedgehog in your garden? My father sent me a mother and two babies, preceded by a peremptory telegram: 'Hogs on train. Collect immediately.' But within a week they had disappeared in spite of loving little offerings of dead beetles, grubs, and dog meat."

I didn't know either, so I asked, and discovered what a hard life hedgehogs have. They hibernate for half the year and when they rouse in the spring they are sexually aroused too. But mating is tricky (all those spines) and takes time.

The babies are born a month later and arrive naked, but within a fortnight they have their first coat of white spines and within a month are fully clothed and ready to go out at night.

Most of them have poor eyesight but good hearing. They shuffle around in the dark hunting for food. They like beetles, caterpillars and earthworms, and they will walk two miles in a night in search of a good meal. They are flea-ridden, but it is not catching because these are very special fleas and only like the taste of hedgehogs' blood. Hedgehogs can roll themselves up into a ball, prickly spines erect, to keep predators at bay. But they can make little progress against people.

We make their lives a misery. We poison the pests they mean to eat and often poison them too in the process. We dig swimming pools in which they drown. We sweep away the leaves in which they hoped to make their nests, and we make bonfires of the very woodpiles beneath which they had planned to spend the winter. And if they do manage to survive all that, we run them over and kill around 100,000 a year.

Most people have a great affection for hedgehogs, perhaps ever since they read *The Tale of Mrs Tiggy-Winkle*. Lucie, you will recall, didn't like to sit too near Mrs Tiggy-Winkle because all through her gown and her cap there were hair-pins sticking out. Incidentally, the Wildlife Hospital Trust's special hedgehog unit at Aylesbury is called St Tiggy-Winkle's. Try not to wince.

Prickly or not, hedgehogs deserve a warm welcome. Food comes first, but not bread and milk. Bread does nothing for them and milk upsets their stomachs. They like tinned catfood and dog-food as well as liver, raw mince, offal and chicken, but no pork; to them that borders on cannibalism. They drink only water and they prefer to eat in private, at night, with no one watching.

Given a pile of dry leaves they can make themselves at home, but in Avon, the British Trust for Conservation Volunteers has been encouraging people to build a hedgehog house.

They say it must be of untreated wood, because hedgehogs hate the smell of creosote. It should be a box about a foot high with a floor and a roof and a sloping entrance big enough for a hedgehog to get in without lowering his spines. It can be covered with soil and dead leaves and then with a polythene sheet, but it must have a breathing pipe.

Planning permission is not necessary and if you have a hedgehog house in the garden the chances are the hedgehog and her family will stay.

You might even get on speaking terms.

Best Kept with rough edges
❦ ❦ ❦

THE ONE AND only time I helped to judge a Best Kept Village competition I was all for giving every village which had entered a prize. They were all immaculate. Every verge trimmed, every litter bin emptied, every white line painted. The road signs were legible, the bus shelters spotless, the churchyards heavenly.

It is as if we were on a royal visit, said a fellow judge. A royal visit to Trumpton or Camberwick Green, said another.

Only one of our party was silent. He was the oldest among us and, I suspect, the only genuine countryman. Finally he spoke.

It is all too tidy, he said.

His words came back to me years later when I discovered that in one county in Britain the Best Kept Village competition had included a special award for untidiness. Not the untidiness of man, but the untidiness of nature. This is a cry for the conservation of wildlife.

Farmers are frequently accused of pursuing profit at the cost of wildlife but, as *Farmers Weekly* pointed out, wildlife is frequently forgotten in the pursuit of the well-kept look which urbanises even the most rural village. If the village is the winner, is the wildlife the loser?

This was the dilemma which inspired those who put up the special award for the conservation of wildlife in a well kept village. They feared that those villages which had gone out of their way to conserve wildlife might not have been deemed tidy enough to win a main award. So they were judged separately.

The special-award judges were instructed to look for evidence of conscious and positive efforts to attract and protect natural flora and fauna within the village envelope. And that envelope, as they called it, included highway verges, village greens and playing fields, churchyards, schools and libraries, open spaces around inns and shops, factories and farms and, of course, gardens.

They also looked for evidence that nesting sites and potential nesting sites had been left undisturbed and that bird boxes and bat boxes were provided. They looked for areas where food plants for birds and butterflies grew, for a richness and diversity of naturally occurring wild flowers, and for the absence of the use of chemicals. In other words they looked for the real countryside. But ought not the Best Kept Village to be precisely that? Is that not the real meaning of conservation?

Even on my one excursion into judging, and that must be 15 years ago, we were advised to look for the preservation of flora and fauna, and reminded that a well cut verge may be destroying wild flowers before they have time to seed.

Best Kept should mean the removal of man's errors, not the extinction of nature's wonders. No beer cans in the hedgerows but plenty of berries.

The man who dreamed up the special award believes not only that hedges should be cut in an A-shape to encourage nesting but that we should not be in too much of a hurry to tidy up broken and fallen trees. As long as it is not hazardous, he says, timber should be left to encourage insects and flora.

The old gentleman who thought his fellow judges too tidy-minded would have agreed with all of that. He liked to see gates mended, stiles safe, stone walls intact, but he also liked to see patches of nettles and rosebay willowherb.

Only the other day I drove through the village that we chose that year as the Best Kept. A row of plaques on the wall of the village hall had signalled that it has continued over the years to persuade the judges of its diligence. It is still beautifully manicured. What it lacks are the rough edges.

More and more villages and villagers are beginning to realise that you can overdo it. They are setting aside special areas for wildlife. But that too is a symptom of the same fastidiousness.

What we wanted to see, said the man who ran the special award scheme, is not one area set aside for wildlife but provision made for it throughout the village. Which is as it used to be; and can be again.

When the special award for wildlife conservation in a village was made and presented, and others heard about it, they were inspired to do the same. But I hope they keep quiet about it.

The last thing a winning village wants is a horde of visitors trampling over the place. It is when Best Kept becomes Most Visited that the damage is done.

That is why I have carefully refrained from identifying the county in which this new award was made. I shall not even whisper its name.

As the Owl said to the Pussycat, this is between us.

Vote conservatory

❧❧❧

FROM NOW ON I shall vote Conservatory. In the past I have voted Lean-to and even Folly, but no longer. I have been extended, or rather converted. I have discovered that a conservatory is something more than an extension to a home; it is a conversion to a new way of life.

I read somewhere that a conservatory ought not to be confused with a greenhouse or a sun room. In a greenhouse the plants come first. In a sun room the people take precedence. But in a conservatory both plants and people blossom.

A greenhouse is a place of work, a solitary cell, in which the dedicated gardener can talk to his or her plants uninterrupted by casual enquiries or social chatter. Visitors are rarely welcome.

A sun room is simply an extra room in the house, or, as estate agents say, an extra reception room, in which the roof is usually solid and any plants no more than decoration. It might even have television.

But a conservatory is for people and plants alike; not any old plants nor for that matter any old people, but for special plants and for people who take a delight in them, and in each other.

The Romans had greenhouses, the Tudors had orangeries, but it was the Victorians who took to the convervatory. One of the first, and one of the most beautiful, was built at Chatsworth in the 1830s and it greatly impressed Queen Victoria when she came to call.

It was designed by Joseph Paxton, a farmer's son, who went on to design the Great Exhibition Building of 1851, which was erected in Hyde Park and then dismantled, moved to south London, and re-erected as the Crystal Palace. It burned down in 1936, but there is now a replica in Dallas – where else?

The Chatsworth Conservatory inspired the great Palm House at Kew, which is still there and has just been renovated. Indeed, when I was in the Palm House interviewing the man in charge of renovation I decided I too must have a conservatory – albeit somewhat smaller. A similar thought struck countless Victorians. First the rich industralists, like Lord Leverhulme, copied the upper classes and built themselves conservatories, then the prosperous middle classes did the same. Hothouses for the millions, said the advertisements, and conservatories sprang up alongside thousands of villas.

But the First World War did for them. The upkeep was too expensive and in the Twenties and Thirties many were allowed to fall down. (They blew up the one at Chatsworth, at the fifth attempt.) The conservatory was slow to come back. Garden sheds and greenhouses were popular in the Sixties, and then gradually in the Seventies the conservatory began to appear.

In the Eighties nothing could stop it. There are now even more conservatories being erected than there were in the Edwardian age.

But there are villains. A friend of mine, seduced by an advertisement in a respectable journal, paid £1,200 deposit on a conservatory and has yet to see a pane of glass. It is not worth suing, said her solicitor, because it will cost her more than that to get her money back.

As in all such matters it is wise to deal only with the reputable and always to take the best-informed advice. It helps to have a friendly architect and a local builder you trust.

Once up, the conservatory is a delight. Ever since ours went up we have witnessed flowers bloom that we have never seen before – not only passion flowers and oleander, but *Clivia miniata*, *Tibouchina urvilleana*, *Rhodochiton atrosanguineum*, and ones with even longer names.

And that is only the half of it. A conservatory is not so much an extension of the house as a welcome incursion into the garden. Even in fine summers, there are days when we can scarcely sit outside. But in a conservatory you can be in the garden all day and every day, enjoying the plants outside every bit as much as the plants inside, watching the garden unfold. And the seasons, I can't wait for the winter snow.

It is not an exaggeration to say that the conservatory has transformed our lives. It has given a whole new meaning to the phrase "living in the country".

Cottages like ours with thick walls and small windows were built like that because country people in previous centuries had quite enough of the outdoor life working. They sought warmth and shelter in their homes.

A conservatory offers the best of both worlds, indoors and outdoors. I shall vote for the party that says everyone should have one.

Forget the hobgoblins
🍎 🍎 🍎

PUT THAT LIGHT out, said the air-raid warden.

Why? I asked, looking at him with the unblinking stare that only small boys can achieve.

Because there is a war on, he said.

Where? I asked, pushing my luck. Smack.

Here, he said, knocking my turnip lantern to the ground. The candle went out, and that was the first and last time I celebrated Hallowe'en.

It was 31 October 1939 and I had been evacuated to Cumberland. Back home in Newcastle, nobody at school or Sunday school had ever mentioned Hallowe'en to me, not even by its proper title, All Hallows' Eve. All we thought about as October approached November was Bonfire Night. We were forbidden to beg in the streets (no demanding "a penny for the guy") but we ran errands for weeks beforehand to get money for fireworks. In 1939, of course, fireworks too were forbidden. The air-raid warden who extinguished my turnip lantern would have exploded himself if we had lit a bonfire and set off rockets.

In any case, my mind was on other things. It was a farmer's daughter at the village school who first told me about Hallowe'en, witches and warlocks, and I rushed home to learn more about it.

The farmer's wife with whom I was staying knew about things that went bump in the night. By the flickering light of an oil lamp she told me about Hallowe'en.

When I was a girl, she began, (and I knew I was back in the previous century) Hallowe'en and Burns' Night were the two most important nights of the year.

She had been brought up on the Scottish border and she went on to explain how on Hallowe'en there were always bonfires. The old people would talk about the deceased, whose souls were thought to be present; the young would talk about romance.

Every teenage girl would place two nuts beside the bonfire – one representing herself, the other a suitor. If both nuts burned brightly together a marriage was likely, but if one cracked and jumped away, it was all off.

It struck me that her husband, who at the age of 65 thought nothing of standing on his head in the local pub in exchange for glasses of rum, must have been a tough nut, but I kept silent. I asked her instead, why 31 October, why not some other date? And she spoke not of the Eve of All Hallows but of New Year's Eve. It was the last day, she said, of the Old Year.

At the village school the next day the headmaster explained that both the Celts and the Saxons celebrated 31 October as the last day of the year, the day when herds returned from pasture and new tenancy agreements were drawn up.

In that case, I argued, the first of November ought to be a holiday.

And that is how I came to have to write an essay (a composition as we called it then) on Hallowe'en. I also made my first and only turnip lantern; so too, I think, did everyone else in the class, if not the school. But the air-raid warden would have none of them, and next Hallowe'en I was at grammar school with my mind on higher things.

Hallowe'en, however, is making a return, not only as an excuse for children's games but as an opportunity for adult folly. One church group has complained that Hallowe'en is now "the innocent face of superstition and occultism", that dabbling in such foolish pastimes as horoscopes, tarot cards and ouija boards is the first step down an occult path that can only do harm.

Some church leaders say they are alarmed at the number of people who see their lives as being subject to the movement of the planets and the fall of cards.

As Christians we need to strike in prayer on All Hallows' Eve against those dark powers, said one excitable bishop recently.

I am sure, he was quoted as saying, that the Churches welcome any warnings about the demonic forces which people may inadvertently contact when they think they are just dabbling with the paranormal.

A remark which would appear to suggest that he is as daft as they are. I think it would be better to give them a turnip lantern each and tell them not to be so silly.

I am tempted to do the same to those children who come to the door on Hallowe'en demanding "Trick or Treat". That practice, with its hint of infant mugging, comes from the United States. Irish immigrants there took to getting up to mischief on Hallowe'en, causing damage and insisting on payment before they would desist. Now children get treats before they can get up to their tricks, but it still has a hint of harassment about it.

Better the practice on Punkie Night in the village of Hinton St George in Somerset, where on the last Thursday in October, which may or may not be Hallowe'en, the children call at all the houses and ask for candles. With the candles they make their own turnip lanterns – "punkies" they call them – and then they parade around the village singing: "It's Punkie Night tonight". Not long ago somebody – perhaps an air-raid warden out of his time – tried to put an end to this annual parade, but the villagers insisted that it continue.

For the rest of us, probably the best way to celebrate Hallowe'en is to join those who use it as an occasion to make a donation to UNICEF, the United Nations' Children's Fund, and to forget about the hobgoblins.

5

Bats

and

Belfries

A climate for the connoisseur
❦ ❦ ❦

NOVEMBER IS LIKE no other month. It adds up to nothing. Indeed when I was a child, parlour tenors were very fond of a melancholy song (a setting, I think, of a poem by Thomas Hood) which spoke of:

No sun — no moon!
No morn — no noon
No dawn — no dusk — no proper time of day . . .
No shade, no shine, no butterflies, no bees,
No fruits, no flowers, no leaves, no birds — November!

At the time I thought it was a bit exaggerated, and why, I wanted to know, did it not say "no leaves, no trees" to rhyme with bees? I have never really liked November since. And I suspect that I am not alone.

It is a dead month, with autumn gone and spring an age away. We cannot even get away from it; it is too late to sightsee and too early to ski. All we can do is to moan about it, and we do. November is the month when the weather becomes not the small change of conversation, but the rate of exchange.

The British talk about it all year round. It is the introduction to most encounters, but it is a courtesy, not an indictment. It is also a compliment. If we lived in a country where the seas froze over in winter, or the crops withered in the ground in the summer sun, we would not engage in such idle chatter. It would be very serious, a matter of life and death.

But our climate is so moderate, the changes are so subtle, that centigrade (or Celsius, as they now insist on calling it) is too crude a measure for such Fahrenheit refinement. (It is true we have the coldest houses in Europe, but that is our incompetence, not nature's curse.) Ours is a climate for the connoisseur, for whom a shower is an excitement, a sunny interval a content.

It does, however, make life difficult for the weather forecaster. In the United States, where rain is "precipitation" and the weather can be characterised in broad continental sweeps, forecasting must be child's play. Here, the weathermen (with some of whom I am in daily communion) know what is going to happen, but cannot reduce that knowledge to one paragraph. Our weather is an infinite variety of much the same.

We dramatise this subtlety by pretending that the weather is not what it was. When we were young, we all say, every summer was a sequence of sunny days. I spent the first year of the war in the Eden Valley, where the annual rainfall is 30 inches, but I cannot recall a single wet day.

Discussion of the weather also perpetuates the north/south divide. If it snows in the south-east of England, it is a national emergency. If it snows in the north-west it is an insignificant local difficulty. And, as a friend of mine recently pointed out, if rain stops play in the Old Trafford Test, it is Manchester's fault; if it stops play at Lord's it is simply the weather.

In truth we are immoderately fond of our moderate weather, except in November, and we always have been. Pelagius, the fourth-century monk, was the first British writer and conversationalist to emerge from the ancient mists, and he spoke well of our weather. St Augustine of Hippo described him as "bull-necked, full-faced, broad-shouldered, corpulent, and slow-moving like a tortoise weighed down with porridge". I don't think he liked him.

But Pelagius dismissed Augustine's guilty conception of original sin. In London and in Bath, he said, he had not experienced such strange lusts and passions as Augustine had in Carthage, and he thought St Augustine might have "burned less" if he had experienced the cool daily rain of the West Country.

But in November even Pelagius's spirits sank, and he was tempted to go to Rome. There is something about the damp in this dank month which enters the soul, and it is not the gentle dew of heaven. It is a dead hand, as if everything has stopped.

Thank goodness Christmas is coming.

Dusk's redemption
❦ ❦ ❦

WHERE WERE YOU during National Bat Week? asked a friend much given to good causes. It was not like you to be silent, he added.

I was reading, I replied, about bats.

And I was. I received books and booklets about bats by every post during Bat Week, most of them claiming to be the first to tell the truth about the world's most misunderstood mammal. And I read the lot.

You missed your chance; it's too late now, said my friend.

But he is wrong. Now is the hour. Bat time is dusk, and dusk redeems this time of year. Not of course in the city, where the fading light in the early evening simply adds to the torment of the rush hour. But in the country, when the earth is still and the light diminished, dusk is the time to contemplate the bat.

You will know one when you see one, but giving it a name is not easy. It might be the long-eared or the mouse-eared, the lesser horseshoe or the greater horseshoe, barbastelle or pipistrelle, noctule or natterer's. It is difficult to tell precisely in the fading light.

It could even be a Bechstein's bat, which I have always imagined can probably play the piano.

The pipistrelle is the smallest bat in Britain. You could fit one in a matchbox. It weighs no more than 10 paperclips and is only half an inch thick from front to back.

The mouse-eared bat is the biggest in Britain, and the most rare. With that name I had expected it to be common but in fact it could even be extinct. Because, according to one of the books I read, the last representative of the species was born in Britain in 1972. And no one has seen another.

Bats have long had a bad press, perhaps because they seemed to be neither one thing nor the other, but half bird and half animal, and seen only at dusk.

"Suspicions amongst thoughts," wrote Francis Bacon, "are like bats amongst birds, they ever fly by twilight."

William Blake put it more disturbingly:

The bat that flies at close of eve
Has left the brain that won't believe.

In truth, most of the things that we believe about bats are untrue. Blind as a bat is a nonsense. Bats can see perfectly well. They cannot distinguish colours but at dusk they don't need to. They seldom inhabit belfries, and they do not get caught in your hair.

Bats are delicate, warm-blooded, social mammals, not unlike us. A mother bat has one baby a year, which is delivered upside down, fed on milk and looked after in a nursery.

What is remarkable about bats is their sonic sense, the system of echo-location which enables them to find their way about in the dark and locate flying insects, which they then devour. They are nature's most effective insecticide.

What they do is shout out and then listen to the echoes as the sound bounces back. The speed of the return indicates the proximity of the object, the quality of the echo indicates the texture of the object.

Echo calls are very complex, made up of many different sounds and many different frequencies. They are often very loud but we cannot hear them because they are usually at frequencies well above our range of hearing – though you can now buy electronic bat detectors and tune in to their nocturnal chatter.

Long-eared bats never speak above a whisper; horseshoe bats talk through their noses. Some moths can hear bat calls and buzz off when bats are hunting, as moths are the bat's favourite food.

Professor J D Pye explained all this in a set of verses which began:

In days of old and insects bold
(Before bats were invented)
No sonar cries disturbed the skies
Moths flew uninstrumented.

The Eocene brought mammals mean
And bats began to sing;
Their food they found by ultrasound
And chased it on the wing.

Since the passing of the Wildlife and Countryside Bill in 1981, which protected all species of bat, interest in them has increased hugely. Bat lectures, bat seminars and bat walks are very popular. So, too, is the provision of bat boxes. Bats can roost in almost any nook or cranny, but as they are often the inadvertent victims of chemical warfare, they are frequently glad of alternative accommodation.

A bat box is very like a bird box, but the entrance should be not a hole in the front but a slot in the bottom. Bats prefer that way in. The wood of the box should be unplaned, untreated, and at least three-quarters of an inch thick.

Location, however, is even more important than design. Bat boxes work best in coniferous woodland where few alternative roosting places exist. Try one, or better still two or three, in the garden, and don't be offended if no bats show up. You may have to wait several years before you get any lodgers, though my friend who accused me of ignoring Bat Week swears that he found no fewer than 40 bats in one box.

I hope, I said, that you read them a bedtime story before they dropped off. To sleep, that is, to sleep.

Muddied waters
❦ ❦ ❦

ONCE UPON A time there was an old night news editor on a morning newspaper in the north of England who knew Bradshaw, the railway timetable, off by heart. He could direct a reporter from almost any railway station in Britain, mainline or local, to any other, at any time, and on any day, from memory. I may not be educated, he used to say, but I am well-informed.

He was. He could also recite the name of every river that runs down to the sea in Britain, starting at the Mersey and working his way right round the coastline past John o'Groats and Land's End until he came back to the Dee.

Why do you bother to remember them all? I once asked him, in my educated innocence.

Because, my boy, he said, rivers are the most important feature of the landscape.

Wordsworth, you may recall, wrote 34 sonnets about the River Duddon alone, which makes the neglect and the abuse of rivers since his day all the more deplorable.

I suppose people have always to some extent abused rivers – dipped their dirty feet in them, washed their dirty clothes in them, dropped unmentionable things in them. But they have also fished in them, swum in them, and passed their evenings on their banks, entranced by the clear water. Tales From The Riverbank was a television recollection of nursery happiness.

I cannot be alone in always being pleased to see the names of rivers spelled out on motorway signs. For it is as important to know the names of the rivers you are crossing as it is to know the names of the towns you are bypassing.

It is not idle curiosity. It is vital knowledge for anyone with a love of the countryside. Rivers are, or were, essentially refreshment – their running water a signal of the abundance of nature, new every morning. Until we got greedy and careless.

It was very clever to use the power of the running stream to turn the wheels of an Industrial Revolution, but very foolish both to use the water and then to abuse the water.

So much filth was poured into rivers in the last century that people turned their backs on them. The River Irwell, which flows through Manchester, ought to have been as central to the city as the Thames in London or the Liffey in Dublin. But it was so dirty that it slipped through the city behind the backs of the cotton warehouses, out of sight and out of mind.

A hundred years ago a Royal Commission looked into the condition of the Irwell and almost threw up. The river was already a sewer and it got worse.

A few years ago I was involved in the making of a film about the cleaning up of the Mersey Basin, of which the Irwell is part, and I persuaded a group of children to recite a little verse well known to their great grandparents.

> *If with a stick you stir well*
> *The poor old River Irwell,*
> *Very sick of the amusement*
> *You will very soon become;*
> *For foetid bubbles rise and burst.*
> *But that is really not the worst,*
> *For little birds can hop about*
> *Dry-footed on the scum.*

What's changed? asked a nine-year-old, after the recitation.

And he had a point. Fewer factories now discharge directly into the river. Sewage treatment is improved, though there is still much to be done. There are even fish upstream.

But there are new pollutants – new pesticides washing off the fields, new chemicals leaking into the sewers. And always excuses.

Every day the Mersey estuary, for instance, receives 135 million gallons of everything nasty spilling into a wide shallow basin with only a narrow outlet to the sea. In Liverpool they reckon that if you fall into the Mersey you will be poisoned before you can drown. And they reckon it will cost £2,000,000,000 to clean up the thousand miles of waterway, much of it in the countryside, that makes up the Mersey Basin.

But a start has been made, and not before time.

A river should be clean from its source to the sea. Geographers argue that a river is both a conveyor belt and a graving tool. Its aim is to carve for itself a gently sloping course which is smooth and unclogged, and to carry the debris to the ocean.

But it is not a water chute for the wantonly discarded. It should not be a handy receptacle for slops and filth, which foul the water and kill the fish.

To understand some of the hazards to this planet requires scholarship knowledge, but you do not need a degree in chemistry or physics to know when water is dirty. You can see it and you can smell it.

So perhaps we ought each to adopt a river. Perhaps we should have organisations like the Friends of the Lake District, or even the Friends of the M6, to befriend rivers and to make clear to those in authority that enough is enough.

We have muddied and robbed the water for two centuries but we should know better now. We should patrol the rivers from their source to the sea and repel the offenders, determined to go clean and wet into the next century.

That would be a good tale from the riverbank.

More than a place of worship

EVERY MONDAY evening I take a train from Macclesfield to London. I stand on Platform 2 at Macclesfield station looking up at the clock tower of the Church of St Michael and All Angels, the oldest church in the town.

I hear the clock strike a quarter to six but rarely six o'clock because the 17·51 to London Euston is seldom late. When the train arrives I climb aboard, and with a farewell glance at the spire of St Paul's Church, which is on the opposite side of the track, I settle down for the journey.

It takes just over two hours, and in that time the train passes no fewer than 48 churches, whose spires and towers punctuate the landscape.

Looking at them every week, I am reaffirmed in my belief that churches are the essential buildings of England. They are the visible sign of the continuity of our history. Almost everything else we have built is transient, liable to be replaced when it has ceased to be of use. And that was always true.

A church is different. It is both ancient and modern. It is a monument to everything that went before and a promise of what is to come.

However old and fascinating its architecture, however populated its graveyard, it is still what it has always been – a place of worship. People go to church, as they have always gone, to pray, to celebrate, to be baptised, confirmed, wed. And to depart this life.

And they go to *their* church, the church in their village or their parish. And their church is unique. They all are. No two churches are alike, not even two built at roughly the same time. You can see that at a glance, even from a passing train. And closer inspection confirms that every church is an individual.

How could it be otherwise? In the Middle Ages a village church was essentially the creation of the local community. It was literally their pride and joy. Often the finished building was far bigger than the local population would appear to require, but it was built not only for the greater glory of God, but also to outshine that of the neighbouring village.

The church was more than a place of worship. It was for gatherings of all kinds, including feasts and dances and miracle plays. In times of trouble it was also a place of refuge.

Every church had, and has, its own history. When I was a schoolboy in Newcastle, I used to cycle round Northumberland looking for the oldest and most interesting churches.

My favourite, I recall, was the church of St Mary the Virgin on Lindisfarne, Holy Island. The church stands next to the ruins of the Benedictine monastery and is overlooked by a wonderful statue of St Cuthbert.

I was also very fond of the Church of St Michael and All Angels at Ford, partly because it is even older than the castle next to it, and partly because you can see the site of the Battle of Flodden Field from it.

In the Lake District I am always torn between Martindale and Matterdale.

St Peter's Church in Martindale is a thousand feet above sea level and must be one of the highest and loneliest churches in England.

The 16th-century church at Matterdale has no saint to its name. It is undedicated, perhaps because it was built at the insistence of the local people, who had grown weary of walking all the way to Greystoke church every Sunday.

Nowhere is there a St Monday's Church. But in Burnley there is a St Monday Festival.

Don't bother to look up St Monday in a hagiography. He never existed. But when a weaver in Burnley had too much to drink on a Sunday night he would take Monday off, arguing that it was St Monday, a holy day or holiday. Not so much the Feast of the Passover as the Feast of the Hangover.

At the St Monday Festival I heard all about the campaign to

save St Peter's, the oldest church in Burnley. In January 1989 it was closed because it was in imminent danger of collapse. But the people would not let it fall down.

They raised the money not only to preserve it but to make sure that in future they will be able to use it as a place of worship and for gatherings of all kinds, just as their ancestors did.

And rightly so.

There are, of course, those who argue that money spent on restoring churches would be better spent on the poor. Judas made that very point when a woman anointed Jesus with very expensive perfume in an extravagant gesture of faith and love.

Jesus reproved him. You will always have the poor, you will not always have me, was the gist of his reply.

Theologians have argued about it ever since. A friend of mine was similarly torn when deciding whether or not to attend the Symphony for the Spire of Salisbury Cathedral.

He decided that the Cathedral, too, is an extravagant gesture of faith and love, a word of God that speaks of the quality of life. So he bought a ticket, though he was still troubled.

I shall try to enjoy the Symphony with a clear conscience, he said, for I suspect that if we do not value such places of beauty, which refresh the human spirit, then we shall lose not only our cathedrals but also the vision and the will to help the poor.

I would go further. I would add that we should also lose something of ourselves and of our identity.

I cannot see Salisbury Cathedral from my train but I can see Lichfield Cathedral. And when I reach London I make my way to my flat in the Barbican, from the bedroom of which I can see the Church of St Giles, Cripplegate, where Oliver Cromwell was married.

Then I go through to the sitting room and look out at St Paul's Cathedral, reassured that everything is in its right place.

Rite and festive
❦ ❦ ❦

IN THE WEEK before Christmas, in the year in which I was three, I got up early one morning and went downstairs to find the rooms hanging with Christmas decorations. I ran back upstairs and into my parents' bedroom.

The fairies, I announced, have been to our house.

My mother recounted this incident on many subsequent occasions, much to my embarrassment, but in my innocent enthusiasm I had touched upon a truth – that Christmas is both pagan and Christian.

Christmas Day itself, 25 December, is the day of the winter solstice and was chosen by the Church in AD440 precisely because it had always been a time of festival for heathen people. In Anglo-Saxon England it was New Year's Day.

The Romans celebrated the Festival of Saturn in December and decorated the temples with greenery. The Saxons used holly and ivy; the Druids mistletoe. And the early Christians gathered all these together to decorate the church at Christmas.

The Romans are also said to have decorated fir trees, but the decorated Christmas tree did not reach England until 1840. It and Santa Claus arrived from Germany after Queen Victoria had married her Prince Albert.

The Germans had always celebrated the feast of Santa Nikolaus (St Nicholas) on 6 December, and "good children" had been given small presents the night before. But it was not long before children in every Christian country were hanging up their stockings on Christmas Eve, confident that Santa Claus would arrive on a sleigh pulled by reindeer and fill them with presents.

Christmas cards arrived in Britain soon after Santa Claus. A painter called Dobson is said to have sent the first in 1844, and the first commercial card was produced two years later. Temperance groups condemned it for it showed people drinking, but within 30 years everyone had started sending them.

And all these trappings – the decorations, the cards, the tree, the stockings and the presents – are as much a part of Christmas as carols, and cribs, and midnight mass. Though you should not have the one without the other. First the Silent Night, then the noisy day.

There is even a pagan silence associated with Christmas – mumming. A mummer is an actor who cannot speak, but he is not as subtle as a mime, and the odd sound of anguish or merriment may escape from his lips.

Mumming is a midwinter enterprise, an activity which preceded Christianity, and which is connected with fertility rites, when in the darkest days of winter people fear the death of the year and hope that spring will come again. In a mummers' play there is usually a death, a challenge and a resurrection.

The best mummers, or so I am told for I have never seen them perform, are to be found in Gloucestershire, where the Waterley Bottom Mummers appear in several villages around Christmas. And at Marshfield, also in Gloucestershire, another company of mummers always performs on Boxing Day. Seven characters, dressed anonymously in strips of paper, are introduced by the Town Crier. A sword fight follows in which King William kills Little Man John, who is brought back to life by Doctor Phoenix in time for a song and dance.

At the village of Crookham, near Aldershot in Hampshire, mummers also perform on Boxing Day. They too have seven characters, but only five are dressed in strips of paper. The Doctor wears a frock coat and a top hat, and Father Christmas wears a traditional red robe and a white beard. He is killed by Johnny Jack but he is not brought back to life by the Doctor, and nobody in Crookham, I am told, knows why that should be. But nobody would dream of changing the plot.

On Christmas Eve, in the Yorkshire mill town of Dewsbury, they ring the bell in the parish church once for every year of Our Lord. They do it every year to remind the Devil of his defeat by Christ's birth, death and resurrection. They hope that by doing it the Devil will keep well away from Dewsbury for the next 12 months. Which I suppose makes it an act of piety with a hint of superstition.

But why do they do it in Dewsbury and, as far as I know, nowhere else in Britain? According to the local legend – and there is no written evidence for this but everyone in Dewsbury swears that it is true – a man called Thomas de Soothill, a rich man, killed his servant. As an act of penance he gave a bell to the parish church with the request that it should be rung on Christmas Eve forever to remind him of his crime.

The bell is known as Black Tom of Soothill. Its lengthy ring on Christmas Eve is one of two very odd English church customs at Christmas. The other is at Aldermaston, once every three years. This is the candle auction. It is the auction of a piece of land known as the Church Acre. A horseshoe nail is driven into a tallow candle about an inch from the top. The candle is lit and the vicar invites bids. The bidding continues until the candle burns down and the nail drops out. The successful bid is the last one before that happens, and the winner then becomes the tenant of Church Acre for the next three years and pays the amount of his bid as his annual rent. It is clearly an improvement on the community charge. Throughout the candle auction, until the nail drops out, the bidders spend the time drinking rum and smoking church warden pipes.

All these antics, it seems to me, add to the festivities, without diminishing the essential message of Christmas. God rest ye merry, as the carol says.

In tune with the words
❧ ❧ ❧

WHY IS IT, asked a colleague in London, that carols singers only know one carol – *Good King Wenceslas* – and they only know the first verse of that? Not where I live, I replied. They not only know all of every carol, they can sing them in five parts.

A good thing, too. What would Christmas be without carols? The question is rhetorical, but the answer is simple: joyless.

The carol, said a great scholar on the subject, gives voice to the common emotions of healthy people in language that can be understood and in music that can be shared by all. It is serious but not solemn, it is joyful and sincere.

They had little time for carols between the fifth century and the 15th. The Church Fathers looked upon such communal singing as frivolous. Francis of Assisi, on the other hand, liked jovial singing and fiddle music and for that matter marzipan. It was he who first installed a crib in a church at Christmas and encouraged children to gather round it and sing.

That was in the 13th century. But it was almost another 200 years, according to the aforesaid scholar, before the carol rose with the ballad, because people wanted something less severe than the old Latin office hymns and more vivacious than the plainsong melodies.

Chaucer's pilgrims were probably among the first English carol singers. The first collector of carols in this country was a grocer called Richard Hill who between 1500 and 1536 wrote down all manner of things that he did not wish to forget – tables of weights, dates of fairs, his children's birthdays, cookery recipes, riddles, puzzles, poems – and carols.

But Cromwell put a stop to all that. In 1644 Christmas Day fell on a Wednesday and the Long Parliament ordered that it be kept not as a feast day but as a fast day. Three years later they abolished Christmas altogether, and Hezekiah Woodward described it as, "The Old Heathen's Feasting Day . . . the

Profane Man's Ranting Day, the Multitude's Idle Day, and the True Christian Man's Fasting Day." No carols for him.

And even after the Restoration of the monarchy the old carols were largely forgotten, except by the poor. The 18th-century gentleman thought himself above such things. And the Wesleys, though they liked the tunes, preferred their own words.

The first modern collection of traditional carols was not published until 1822 by a remarkable man called Davies Gilbert, who was MP for Bodmin, President of the Royal Society and the man who awarded Brunel the contract to build the Clifton Suspension Bridge. But even he spoke of them as a thing of the past. And a second collector, William Sandys, who published *Christmas Carols Ancient and Modern* in 1833, said that the practice of carol singing appeared to get more neglected every year.

Certainly it was in church. The old carols were ignored and there were new carols inspired by the sham Gothic of the late Victorian church buildings – music which, in the words of one scholar, was deplorably easy to write and required little or no skill to perform. Not carols at all, but bad hymns.

But the old carols still lingered in the country. Country children, with only a sketchy knowledge of the words and the tunes, would go from door to door in the weeks before Christmas, but their singing was a form of begging. They were usually paid to shut up and be off, hence the expression "hush money".

But their parents and more often their grandparents remembered the old carols, even if they rarely sang them. And when the church music scholars finally set to work towards the turn of the century to recover both the words and the music of the real carols, they not only looked to the ancient texts but searched the memories of old people in the countryside. And the genuine old traditional carols were re-established.

So when the carol singers come to your door this Christmas, insist they sing the right words to the right tune. And when you go to church, remember, as you join in the singing, that you are bearing witness to a spontaneous and undoubting faith.

Happy Christmas
❦ ❦ ❦

I<small>F</small> I A<small>M</small> invited, as I sometimes am, to read the lesson in our village church at the midnight service on Christmas Eve, I always
hope that it will be Luke, though I know it should be John.
Luke is the story; John is the meaning.

Luke rolls off the tongue. She wrapped him in swaddling
clothes, and laid him in a manger, because there was no place
for them at the inn. The shepherds watched over their flock and
an angel of the Lord appeared to them. We have known it all
since Sunday school.

John is a different matter. In the beginning was the Word,
and the Word was with God, and the Word was God. That is
the theology. The words are simple, but the meaning is difficult
and profound.

People have been reflecting upon those words for 2000
years, but every attempt to improve on them seems to have
moved further from, rather than closer to, the truth. And yet
Christmas is clearly the moment to contemplate their meaning.

The Festival itself has got out of hand. It is true that 25
December was always a festival day among the pagan and the
heathen. In Anglo-Saxon England it was also New Year's Day,
and it is almost certainly not the day on which Christ was born.
But that is no excuse. Present-giving has never been as
profligate, nor the feasting as gluttonous. And we all have to
plead guilty. It is as if people have lost the ability to enjoy each
other's presence, as distinct from each other's presents. But it is
the thought that counts, and church at midnight seems to me to
be essential both to the understanding and to the enjoyment of
Christmas. Otherwise it is simply an indulgence.

Not that we want to be hectored. Nothing is more off-
putting than the evangelical fervour of those who describe themselves as "born-again".

That is simple error; what we are looking for is simple

truth. And we may have to settle for just a glimpse of it, which is the reason for going to church at Christmas.

I make my living asking questions, but there is one question I would never presume to ask anyone, and that is: what do you think about when you are kneeling at the Communion rail? That would seem to me to be an intrusion into private happiness.

I was once asked the question myself and when I thought about it, I decided that I didn't think of anything at that moment in the sense of formulating a proposition, marshalling an argument, or even wondering where I had put the car keys. Although I was on my knees I didn't even pray in the sense of rehearsing a petition or issuing a plea. I simply waited for the wafer and the wine and the repetition of the words "keep you in eternal life".

The words are in the present tense. They are not a promise for the future but a statement about now. And that, I think, is the glimpse of eternity. After that, the walk back to the pew is a passage of re-entry into the temporal world, and back to the mince pies. There is a very moving piece in Evelyn Waugh's novel *Helena*. Helena was the mother of the Emperor Constantine and she travelled to the Holy Land where she discovered the relics of the Cross on which Jesus was crucified, or so they led her to believe.

She reached Bethlehem and there she sat reflecting upon the journey of the Three Wise Men.

"Like me," she said to them, "you were late in coming . . . You are my especial patrons and patrons of all latecomers, of all who have a tedious journey to make to the truth, of all who are confused with knowledge and speculation, of all who stand in danger by reason of their talents."

And then she offers them a prayer. "For His sake who did not reject your curious gifts, pray always for all the learned, the oblique, the delicate. Let them not be quite forgotten at the throne of God when the simple come into their kingdom."

Put that on your Christmas card.

The last word
❦ ❦ ❦

LILAH WAS TALKING to herself.

After all these years, she mewsed, I am glad that I am finally
an only cat. At last I have the place to myself. Sixteen years in
the same household and seldom a day to call my own.

When I first came, I remember, there was a great soft Sandy
thing who always wanted to be cuddled. And there was Scoob,
who was grey and pink, like an old edition of *The Financial
Times*.

He would speak to anyone. The postman, the milkman, even
the window cleaner. How are you, Scooby Doo, they would
say. Ridiculous.

I kept myself to myself, even though I had a brother,
Samson. My full name, you appreciate, is Delilah.

Samson was reckless. He was forever trying to fish frogs out
of the garden pond, and frequently fell in. He would jump on
the bonnet of moving cars and pull faces at the driver. But one
day he missed and was run over.

The Children wept, I remember. I shed a tear, too, but I
didn't let on. In fact I ran away. Himself informed the nation on
the radio. I answered, he said, to the name Lilah Lambcake. I
was mortified. But I came back.

Then Leo arrived. I quite liked him. Somebody had left him
in a lock-up garage without food and drink for three weeks. So
he was skin and bone.

The Children fussed over him. Indeed, they were forever
sticking their faces in ours, muttering endearments. Leo and
Scoob would purr. I scratched.

The Eldest Child, who eventually went off to count monkeys
for a living, said that I should run for Parliament, and even run
the country. I could be called Mrs Scratcher, he said, but I
never got the joke.

Though I did think of going to the country. That was when They arrived.

Himself had got himself appointed President of something called CAT, the Cat Action Trust. It existed, he would say portentously, to solve the problem of the feral cat.

I can hear him now.

Feral cats are domestic cats living wild, he would say. Either because they have strayed from home or, more commonly, because they are unwanted and have been expelled from home, thrown out.

Feral cats do not walk alone, he would rabbit on. They gather in colonies wherever they can find food and shelter. In backyards, on building sites, in hospital gardens, in every urban corner. They are the inhabitants of dereliction. So he rescued two, from a Town Hall cellar in London. Oscar and Emmy, he called them. Militant Tendency cats if ever I saw some.

They arrived, I recall, on a Good Friday. They were six weeks old and had travelled in a basket from London. They stepped out of the basket, without so much as a by-your-leave, and marched into the house, tails held high like placards.

They did not just make themselves at home; they took over. She was black and white, with a pink nose, and talked non-stop. He was nearly all black, looked like a rug on the move and rummaged all night in the hedgerows. Even Herself called him That Cat.

Myself, I would have nothing to do with them and insisted on eating alone.

Leo and Scoob, old codgers by then, were more accommodating, but I suspect it hastened their end. Though, to be fair, both were in their late teens when they popped off.

But that left me alone with the Terrible Twins. I never had a moment's peace. And was I glad when they went off with the Daughter to live at her farm. From then on, I took sole charge.

From that blessed day to this, I have reminded Himself and Herself regularly of the benefits that I bring to them.

I prevent you, I tell them, from thinking only of yourselves.

When you are depressed, I give you something better to think about – me.

When you are confused or undecided, my timetable determines your day.

When you are troubled, I allow you to stroke me.

When you have something on your mind, I am always there to listen.

I greet you in the morning and wish you God speed at night.

You would be lost without me.

Not that you always appreciate my presence. There was an unfortunate fortnight when you dispatched me to an institution. I was not pleased. As I told you on your return, I did not like being in the slammer. And it will not happen again. I am the Cat in Residence.

Lilah pawsed. And from the kitchen came the sound of Herself. "Lilah, tea time," she called.

"About time too," said Lilah, rising and stretching. "And it had better be fish."

O.P